Towards a Safer
World of Banking

Towards a Safer World of Banking

Bank Regulation After the Subprime Crisis

T.T. Ram Mohan

BEP BUSINESS EXPERT PRESS

Towards a Safer World of Banking: Bank Regulation After the Subprime Crisis

First published in 2017 by
Business Expert Press, LLC
222 East 46th Street, New York, NY 10017
www.businessexpertpress.com

ISBN-13: 978-1-63157-437-5 (paperback)
ISBN-13: 978-1-63157-438-2 (e-book)

Business Expert Press Finance and Financial Management Collection

Collection ISSN: 2331-0049 (print)
Collection ISSN: 2331-0057 (electronic)

Cover and interior design by Exeter Premedia Services Private Ltd., Chennai, India

First edition: 2017

10 9 8 7 6 5 4 3 2 1

Printed in the United States of America.

To the memory of my late father T.T. Vijayaraghavan whose career as a journalist instilled in me a passion for writing and journalism and whose passing has left an enormous void in my life

Abstract

In 2007, the United States faced a financial crisis that severely impacted the U.S. economy as well as the world economy. Indeed, the financial crisis of 2007 has been characterized as the worst since the Great Crash of 1929. The world economy is yet to recover from the impact.

This book seeks to address a number of issues thrown up by the crisis of 2007:

- Why do banking crises happen so often and why is their impact so severe?
- What were the main causes of the subprime crisis?
- In terms of bank regulation, what steps have been taken to prevent such crises in the future and make banking safer?
- Is banking today indeed safer than in 2007? If not, what are the issues that remain to be addressed in regulatory terms?

The book contends that, while several factors can be blamed for the financial crisis of 2007, a failure of regulation was the most important one. After assessing the changes to bank regulation that have happened since, it concludes that these are not good enough to make the banking system considerably safer than before. It argues that we need to look at radical, out-of-the-box solutions if another major financial upheaval is to be prevented.

The book is aimed primarily at students of business management, economics and international economics, and at bank executives. It should also be of interest to general readers who are curious to know what the subprime crisis was all about.

Keywords

bank regulation, banking, banking crises, financial crises, financial sector, financial stability, global financial crisis, subprime crisis

Contents

Foreword

The financial crisis that erupted in the United States in 2007 and that came to engulf the world economy has given rise to a torrent of research and analysis. The underlying motivation is to better understand banking crises so that we can ensure that these hugely disruptive events do not happen.

In this book, which is aimed at undergraduate and graduate students of economics and finance and bank executives, I attempt to summarize our understanding of the financial crisis and to take stock of the measures that have been taken so far to prevent the recurrence of such a crisis.

Chapter 1 examines the record of financial crises. It shows how banks are inherently prone to failure—they are almost designed to fail, as a recent book has claimed. When they do, they impose large costs on the economy. Estimates of these costs vary, depending on the methodology used. A caveat is, however, required here. We assume all too readily that banks are the cause of banking crises. However, in a recent best-selling book, two economists have put forward the provocative view that banking crises have more to do with the buildup of private debt; they are not about banks *per se*.

Chapter 2 explores the causes of the financial crisis of 2007. After examining a dozen explanations, we are inclined to believe that a failure of regulation was the primary cause. We go along with the view that a buildup of private debt was certainly an important cause. However, we would argue that the bursting of this bubble would not have impacted the banking sector and created as much havoc as it did had banking regulation been more effective.

Chapter 3 looks at the proposals put forward or implemented in order to prevent the recurrence of serious financial crises. Many of the measures put in place are useful and should certainly help to both prevent crises and to contain the impact of these. However, we note that they do not adequately address the problem of too-big-to-fail, the fact that large banks cannot be allowed to fail because of the havoc that such failures create.

Chapter 4 looks at possible ways of dealing with the too-big-to-fail problem. We point out that the effectiveness of the steps taken will be known only over time. Perhaps, the answer lies in tackling the problem head-on: preventing banks from getting too big in the first place.

The last chapter, Chapter 5, reviews some of the out-of-the-box solutions proposed by those who believe that the measures taken so far and the proposals currently on the regulators' table just won't do. We put forward our own view that, taking a leaf out of the Indian banking model, perhaps having some government ownership in the banking sector could conduce to stability in banking.

I do hope that the book will help students gain an understanding of the crisis of 2007 and banking crises in general. For bank executives and regulators, the book should serve as a handy guide to what has been accomplished in the realm of bank regulation as well as to unfinished business. It should also provide a better appreciation of managing risk in the banking sector.

Acknowledgments

This book, like much of my professional work, has been made possible with the patience and support of my wife, Jayashree, and the joy provided by our son, Nandu. My mother, Padmini, and my in-laws, Susheela and N.S. Narayan, have always provided encouragement.

I am grateful to Ankit Kariya, Viddhi Kotak, and Raja Mohanty for providing research assistance. Roystan La'Porte, the India representative of Business Expert Press pursued me relentlessly until I yielded to his request to write this book, Scott Isenberg, the Executive Acquisitions Editor, commissioned the book and provided support and guidance. The editorial team of Exeter (India) rendered editing services for the book with unusual promptness and efficiency. To all of them, my deepest gratitude.

The only regret I have is that my beloved father, T.T. Vijayaraghavan, passed away when the book was getting done, and I am not able to share the book with him.

List of Abbreviations

ABCP	Asset Backed Commercial Paper
AIG	America and Insurance Giant
ARMs	Adjustable-Rate Mortgages
BCBS	Basel Study on Banking Supervision
BCRA	Backstop Credit Rating Approach
BHCs	Bank Holding Companies
BIS	Bank for International Settlements
CBO	Congressional Budget Office
CCR	Contribution to Capital Requirement
CDOs	Collateralized Debt Obligations
CDS	Credit Default Swaps
CFMA	Commodity Futures Modernization Act
CoCos	Contingent Convertibles
CRA	Community Reinvestment Act
CRO	Chief Risk Officer
ECB	European Central Bank
FCIC	Financial Crisis Inquiry Commission
FD	Financial Development
FDIC	Federal Deposit Insurance Corporation
FHA	Federal Housing Authority
FHFA	Federal Housing Finance Agency
FNMA	Federal National Mortgage Association
FSOC	Financial Stability Oversight Council
FTC	Federal Trade Commission
GDP	Gross Domestic Product
GNMA	Government National Mortgage Association
GSEs	Government-Sponsored Enterprises
HOEPA	Home Ownership and Equity Protection Act
HOLC	Home Owner's Loan Corporation
HUD	Housing and Urban Development
IPCC	Intergovernmental Panel on Climate Change

LAC	Loss Absorption Capacity
LCR	Liquidity Coverage Ratio
LOLR	Lenders Of Last Resort
MBS	Mortgage-Backed Securities
NIM	Net Interest Margin
NPA	Nonperforming Assets
NRSROs	Nationally Recognized Statistical Rating Organizations
NSF	Net Stable Funding
OCC	Office of Controller of Currency
OLA	Orderly Liquidation Authority
PFAS	Pawnbroker For All Seasons
PSBs	Public Sector Banks
QM	Qualified Mortgage
RoE	Return on Equity
RRBA	Revised Ratings-Based Approach
RSF	Required Stable Funding
SA	Standardized Approach
SBI	State Bank of India
SIFIs	Systemically Important Financial Institutions
SIVs	Structured Investment Vehicles
SRMs	Shared-Responsibility Mortgages
SSFA	Simplified Supervisory Formula Approach
STS	Simple, Transparent, and Standardized
TARP	Troubled Asset Relief Program
TBTF	Too-Big-To-Fail
VaR	Value-at-Risk

CHAPTER 1

Banking Crises

Why Banks Are Fragile

Banks are fragile. They are prone to failure. We know that very well, don't we? Some of the largest banks failed or were on the verge of failure during the financial crisis of 2007. They included some of the best known and respected names in the financial world: Royal Bank of Scotland, Citigroup, Bank of America, and investment banks such as Bear Stearns and Lehman Brothers. Governments had to spend billions of dollars to rescue banks even while letting many fail.

Banks are connected with each other in ways that we shall soon make clear. So the failure of one or more large banks can cause several other banks to fail, leading to a crisis for the banking sector as a whole. And when the banking sector as a whole is in crisis, it tends to drag down the economy. Again, we have come to understand very well the havoc that a banking crisis can create in an economy—the global economy is still struggling to return to the growth path it was on before the crisis.

What is it that makes banks so fragile? Well, the key to bank fragility is the high level of debt—more precisely, the ratio of debt to equity (or "leverage")—at which banks operate. For a manufacturing company, a debt-to-equity ratio of more than, say, 1:1 would be considered high. In shipping, the ratio tends to be higher, say, 4:1. It can be even higher in infrastructure sectors, such as roads and ports. In banking, we have been willing to tolerate a debt-to-equity ratio of 30:1 and even higher.

Students of finance would know that as the ratio of debt to equity rises, the probability of failure (or "bankruptcy") rises. As debt rises, so does the interest that the firm has to service. More and more of the firm's income goes toward servicing the interest burden. As a result, even a small drop in income could mean an inability to service debt. The extraordinary leverage at which banks operate is thus the source of fragility in banking.

Why banks are allowed to be so fragile is a matter of debate. One argument made for the high leverage allowed to banks is that debt is less costly than equity. Debt also carries tax benefits whereas equity does not. The post-tax cost of debt is, therefore, considerably lower than that of equity. When banks are allowed a high debt-to-equity ratio—the argument goes—the total cost of capital for banks becomes lower than it would be otherwise.

The cost of capital of a bank has implications for the rate at which it lends. If we view the lending rate as the sum of three elements—the cost of capital, the cost of operations, and a profit margin—then it should be obvious that keeping the cost of capital low translates into a lower lending rate for borrowers. Investment in an economy is inversely proportional to the lending rate. The lower the lending rate, the greater the investment in the economy and the higher the growth rate.

In short, allowing banks to carry a high level of debt benefits the economy by translating into a higher growth rate. We shall examine this argument critically in Chapter 3. For now, let us stay with the argument and focus on the outcome of permitting extremely high levels of leverage of banking. Let us see what happens when banks operate at a high leverage.

Consider a bank, Bank A, with a balance sheet of a bank as shown as follows:

Liabilities		Assets	
Equity	$10	Loans $100	
Deposits	$90		
	$100		$100

The bank mentioned previously has a leverage of 90/10 or 9:1, which is very modest by the standards of today's banks. Suppose the bank's loans were to fall in value by just 10 percent to $90. What would happen? The equity of the bank would be wiped out, that is, the bank would go bankrupt. Thus, in a portfolio of loans, only a small proportion of loans—in this case 10 percent—needs to go bad for the bank to go bust. This is the outcome of high leverage.

Let's take this a little further. It's not necessary for the value of loans to fall by 10 percent for the bank to fail. Suppose the value of loans falls by 5 percent, so that the value of assets is now $95. If word of this got around, depositors would conclude that the bank was close to failure. They would then start queuing up to take back their money.

To meet the demands of depositors, the bank would have to quickly sell some of its loans to meet the demands of depositors. Here's another problem with banks: Deposits are liquid (the bank has to allow customers to withdraw their deposits whenever they like) but loans are illiquid, that is, they can't be turned into cash easily.

Since the bank is desperate to raise resources to meet the claims of depositors, it would have to resort to a distress sale of loans, that is, loans would have to be sold at steep discounts to the face value. This could easily translate into a further loss to the bank of $5. Thus, a drop in value of just 5 percent could push the bank into bankruptcy if it triggered panic amongst depositors.

Depositors could panic even if they heard bad news about other banks. They might conclude that it was only a matter of time before their own bank was affected. So even bad news about the banking sector could lead to a run on banks. This is what makes banks especially prone to failure.

But the problem does not end with banks that fail. Thousands of nonbanking firms fail every year without our even noticing these. Bank failure is very different in that it has serious repercussions for the economy at large. This is what distinguishes the failure of a bank from that of a nonbanking firm.

Bank Failure Has Negative Externalities

What do we do with a typical firm whose equity is wiped out? We declare it bankrupt. The shareholders get wiped out. Under the bankruptcy process, the assets pass into the hands of creditors. An administrator is appointed who proceeds to liquidate the assets of the firm and distribute the proceeds amongst the shareholders.

We have seen that a bank can get wiped out even with a small decline in the value of its loans. Suppose we were to apply the usual bankruptcy procedure to a failed bank. What would be the outcome?

Well, in the example given earlier, Bank A would recall the $90 in good loans from borrowers and give it back to depositors. Let us suppose that the bank is able to recover the loans in full (we shall see in the following that this may not happen). The depositors would then go to another bank, Bank B, and place this amount with it. Bank B would then look for borrowers to whom it can lend it out.

Let us say it would like to give loans worth $90 to the firms from which Bank A had taken them back. This is not something that can happen instantaneously. Bank B would have to evaluate the borrowers, build relationships, and gradually raise its exposure to the erstwhile borrowers back to $ 90. The whole process—from the liquidation of Bank A to the reconstruction of loans to the borrowers of Bank A by Bank B—would be enormously time-consuming. It would take, say, a couple of years.

And what would we have achieved? In order to uphold the principle of bankruptcy, we would have deprived firms of vital credit of $90 for two years, thus creating disruptions in the economy. While the liquidation process is being completed, the operations of Bank A's borrowers would be adversely impacted. They may not be able to fully service their loans as a result. Some borrowers would not think it worthwhile to repay their loans in full to a bank that has gone bankrupt—why do so when there is nothing more to be derived from the relationship? Hence, the value of Bank A's assets could fall well below $90 and the depositors might end up receiving a lower amount than what they had put into the bank.

The problem is not confined to the Bank A's investors, borrowers, and depositors. Banks are connected to each other in various ways. They are connected through the payments system. One bank's loan could be another bank's deposit. The failure of one bank could thus put other banks at risk. This is called "contagion." Contagion could jeopardize the entire banking system. When one bank fails, it could undermine depositor confidence in other banks and trigger a general run on banks. Contagion thus tends to magnify the externalities associated with bank failure.

This illustrates an important problem with bank failure. It carries large "externalities," that is, it imposes social costs that are greater than the private costs to the bank's investors. It is not just the shareholders and creditors of the failed bank who bear costs; the broader economy is adversely impacted.

There are externalities with the failures of other firms as well. When a car maker fails, it impacts a range of vendors and dealers. But the externalities that go with bank failure are significantly greater. That is why it is difficult for governments to allow a bank—and especially a large bank—to fail. It should be clear now why governments spent enormous amounts during the financial crisis in trying to rescue banks that had failed or were on the verge of failure. Not doing so would have imposed huge costs on economies.

Ways to Preventing Bank Failure and Their Consequences

So, what do we have by way of banking systems? We have created banks that are prone to failure, thanks to their high leverage. However, we must ensure that these fragile institutions do not fail as that would impose large costs on the economy.

This is a tall order because even the possibility or a rumor of failure can push a bank into insolvency. Banks have liabilities in the form of deposits that are highly liquid—anybody can demand their deposits back at short notice. However, the assets they have (mostly or substantially in the form of loans) are illiquid—they cannot be recalled or sold quickly. Banks are run on the assumption that, any given point in time, only a small proportion of depositors wants their money back. The moment this assumption is violated and depositors queue up in large numbers to ask for their depositors, there is every danger of the bank failing.

In order to prevent panic amongst depositors, which can lead to a run on a bank and push it into insolvency, two mechanisms have been devised.

One is deposit insurance. Under this mechanism, deposits up to a certain specified value are insured by a government agency. This gives depositors the confidence that even if a bank fails, their deposits are safe. So they do not have to queue up before a branch or an ATM machine in order to withdraw their money the moment they pick up some rumor or negative information about a bank.

The other mechanism is the central bank acting as the "lender of last resort" to banks that face what is called a "liquidity" problem, that is, they do not have enough cash to give to depositors who want their money back. The central bank steps in to provide cash to a bank that faces a sudden demand for cash from depositors.

Such lending is typically subject to conditions: The bank must be solvent, that is, the value of its assets exceeds the value of its liabilities; the bank must provide acceptable collateral; and a penal interest rate will be charged. These conditions are intended to ensure that banks avail of the lender-of-lost-resort facility very rarely and only when funds are not available from the market.

These two mechanisms should, in principle, have made banking a lot safer. In practice, this has not happened because these mechanisms give rise to what are known as "adverse selection" and "moral hazard." Both these are problems that arise when a contract is to be signed between two parties under conditions of imperfect information.

Adverse selection is, very roughly, the wrong individuals or firms getting selected in the face of imperfect information. For example, if life insurance is available, people who are older have every incentive to sign up unless ways are found to deter them (say, by charging punitive premia for insurance policies or barring people above a certain age from taking insurance).

Moral hazard is imperfect information that causes one party to a contract to behave in ways that are harmful to the other party. For example, if we offer car insurance to somebody, the beneficiary has an incentive to misbehave (by, say, driving rashly) unless ways are found to deter such behavior (charging high premia to those with a record of accidents).

In the case of banking, we can see how the two mechanisms put in place to prevent bank failure—deposit insurance and lender of last resort—can lead to adverse selection and moral hazard. Knowing that these mechanisms exist, and depositors will be taken care of even if the bank fails, adverse selection will take place: undesirable persons can enter the banking sector.

To prevent precisely this, we have chartering or licensing of banks whereby those wanting to set up banks are carefully screened. Starting a bank requires a license. Even in the economies committed to the free market and even while most other sectors of the economy have been deregulated, banking remains an area in which a license is required for starting a bank.

Similarly, we have several regulations that are intended to check moral hazard, the possibility that those given a license to set up a bank will behave in ways that put depositors at risk. Some of these are:

i. Inspection and monitoring of asset quality
ii. Restrictions on exposure to risky assets, such as real estate, stocks, and commodities
iii. Credit concentration norms that limit exposure to facilities to a given borrower
iv. Disclosure norms for the bank's finances and risk exposures
v. Provisioning requirements for assets that require banks to provide for losses on loans, depending on the quality of loans
vi. Minimum net worth requirements for starting a bank
vii. Minimum capital adequacy for a bank which defines how much of assets a bank can acquire in relation to the capital it has

Actions, such as the ones mentioned earlier, that are taken to check moral hazard will also help check adverse selection.

Too Big to Fail

However, despite all these checks, one seemingly intractable problem remains: the too-big-to-fail problem. Once a bank grows beyond a certain size, its managers can take large risks in the knowledge that the bank will not be allowed to fail. Given what we have outlined earlier about the externalities that go with bank failure, regulators and the government would be wary of the damage that would be caused by letting a large bank fail.

While regulators can, in principle, contain risks taken by large banks through actions such as those listed earlier, there are limits to what they can achieve in practice. For one thing, it is difficult for regulators to judge the risks that go with various banking decisions better than the bankers themselves. Second, by the time the risks associated with certain loans become manifest, it is too late for the regulators to respond. How to deal with the too-big-to-fail problem is a challenge that regulators are struggling to come to grips. We address this issue in detail in Chapter 4.

For now, we have to accept that large banks can fail and, when they do, they can often trigger a banking crisis. We have today a fatal chain of causation in banking: high leverage—fragility—deposit insurance-moral hazard——too-big-to-fail—banking crisis. This chain needs to be broken.

Causes of Banking Crises

We have noted that banks are inherently fragile, thanks to their being allowed to operate at a high level of leverage. We also noted that banks are connected to each other in various ways. These two together predispose banking systems to a crisis. Even fear or panic about the state of banks can trigger a banking crisis because fear or panic can turn out to be self-fulfilling.

This implies that a banking crisis can happen quite independently of the fundamentals of an economy. The economy may be doing well. However, any apprehension about a large bank or a set of banks can quickly lead to a banking crisis. The crisis will impose large costs on the economy. This is one view about banking crises. It is known in the literature as the "sunspots" view of banking crises and it suggests that banking crises can occur quite independently of the fundamentals of an economy. ("Sunspots" refer to extrinsic random variables.)

A second view about banking crises is quite the opposite of the first one. This is that banking crises are a consequence, not a cause of macroeconomic problems. The economy suffers a shock and goes into a downward spiral. Firms operating in the economy are impacted adversely as a result. Banks that are exposed to these firms are affected in turn.

A third explanation is that banking crises have to do with bad banking decisions or with poor design of banking systems. Banks may get carried away in making loans. In wanting to grow rapidly, they may ignore or underestimate the risks that go with loans. Most crucially, regulators may design rules poorly partly because banking rules are the result of bargains struck amongst politicians, regulators, and bankers. For instance, the insurance premium for deposit insurance may have been deliberately kept too low. Also the capital that banks are required to hold against their assets. The combination of bad decisions and bad design can cause banking crises.

Let us consider the second and third explanations. If these do not hold, it would be reasonable to conclude that the first explanation, namely, that banking crises are "sunspot" events that can happen quite independently of the other two factors is correct.

It seems intuitively obvious that a weak macroeconomic environment can create conditions for a banking crisis. However, it turns out that while bad economic conditions can indeed lead on to banking crisis, this is not uniformly the case. One case that is often cited is that of the United States and Canada. Both faced the Great Depression. Yet, while the United States saw some 15,000 banks fail, in Canada only one bank failed. One study notes that between 1875 and 1933, the correlation between the failure rates of U.S. banks and firms was a mere 0.24.[1]

Another study looked at the economic record of 23 countries that had experienced one banking crisis in the period 1970–88.[2] The study came to the following conclusions:

- Few countries showed any significant economic decline in the run-up to a banking crisis. In only seven countries was the cumulative decline in real GDP especially large in the three years preceding a crisis. Indeed, for 14 of the 23 countries, there were at least two separate pre-crisis episodes where the cumulative decline in the per capita GDP growth was larger than that observed in the three years before the crisis.
- In only 5 of 22 countries examined is there an episode of an unusually large increase in the rate of inflation in the three years leading up to the crisis; in 17 countries, there are at least two episodes of larger cumulative increases in the rate of inflation between 1970 and the beginning of the crisis.
- Only four countries exhibit an especially large decline in the value of equity in the three years before the crisis.
- There is little support for the thesis that banking crises are preceded by banking booms, that is, runaway growth in credit is what leads on to a banking crisis. In only 6 out of

22 countries examined was the ratio of private credit to GDP
unusually high in the three years preceding a crisis. In 10 out
of 21 countries, there is at least one pre-crisis period in which
the ratio of private credit to GDP grows at an unusual rate
without any crisis occurring in the following three years.

The authors conclude, "Typically, then, only 20 to 30 percent of the
single-crisis economies exhibit unusually large changes in per capital
GDP growth, inflation or real share values within three years preceding
the occurrence of a crisis."

These results are completely counter-intuitive: most of us would think
that a weak economy means weak firms and weak firms could translate
into a banking crisis.

The contrasting experiences of United States and Canada during the
Great Depression illustrate that bad economic conditions by themselves
may not tip an economy into crisis. What may matter is the vulnerability
of a given banking system. Two academics suggest that such vulnerability
may arise from flawed design of banking systems.[3]

The authors looked at 117 countries in the World Bank's Financial Structure Database. Only 34 of those countries (29 percent) were
crisis-free from 1970 to 2010. The authors then sought to ascertain how
many countries were crisis-free and also had abundant credit. (This was
defined as an average ratio of bank credit to GDP one standard deviation
above the mean for the 117 countries in the dataset, which happened to
be 83 percent.) Only three countries met both criteria!

Given that countries stand to benefit from having a stable banking
system and broad access to credit, why would that be so? The authors
postulate that fragility of banking systems and scarcity of credit arise from
faulty design of banking systems. To be more precise, there are conflicts
of interest inherent in banking systems and few governments do a good
job of managing these.

The authors identify three types of conflicts of interest in banking.
First, governments regulate banks and, at the same time, see these as a
source of finance. Second, governments enforce the credit contracts that
bind debtors with banks but they rely on those very debtors for political
support. Third, the government allocates losses among creditors following

bank failures but depends on one set of creditors, bank depositors, for political support.

Banking crises arise from the bargains that are struck in the process of managing these conflicts of interest. It is not as if these crises are the result of unforeseen economic shocks. Similarly, scarcity of credit may be the result of having too few banking players that can profit from scarcity or the government not having regulations that ensure that banks reach up to the unbanked. Both crises and underbanking flow directly from the political structures in economies—it all comes down to who benefits from the way banks are run.

From what we have said earlier, it should be clear that merely because economic crises and banking crises are correlated, one cannot say that it is economic crises that lead to banking crises. Nor does it follow that banking crises are the cause of economic crises. How do we know that lack of supply of credit, arising from problems at banks, is creating problems in the economy? It may well be that the shocks to the economy that cause problems in the banking sector also lead to a fall in investment and output and hence to a fall in demand for credit.

One paper tried to crack this problem.[4] It did so by comparing the effects of banking crises on sectors that were heavily dependent on external finance with the effects on sectors that were less dependent. The former was impacted more severely. It also looked at the effects of banking crises on developing countries that have comparatively less access to external finance (so that firms dependent on external finance would find it difficult to tap funds from abroad). Banking crises tended to be more disruptive in developing countries. The authors concluded that banking crises do have real effects and hence banks need more support in times of financial distress than other commercial enterprises.

An economic crisis may not arise from a banking crisis. It's fair to suggest, however, that once there is a crisis in the economy, a banking crisis will make things worse. Studies cited in the paper mentioned earlier show that credits to the private sector and economic output do decelerate during banking crisis.

In sum, we do not really know for sure whether an economic contraction causes a banking crisis or it is a banking crisis that leads on to an economic contraction. What we can say with a measure of confidence, however, is that a banking crisis exacerbates the effects of a macroeconomic contraction once the latter has happened. The downturn in an economy is sharper than it would have been if banks had not been as fragile as they are.

A recent best-selling book, *The House of Debt*, authored by two economists, Atif Mian and Amir Sufi, provides a totally radical and provocative view of banking crises.[5] The authors argue that banking crises arise not from problems in the banking sector *per se*; they are closely related to large increases in household debt. They examine five big postwar banking crises identified by economists Carmen Reinhart and Kenneth Rogoff (whom we shall cite later in this chapter). These are: Spain in 1977, Norway in 1987, Finland and Sweden in 1991, and Japan in 1992.

Each of these banking crises, the authors found, was preceded by large increases in private debt, that is, the debt of households and nonfinancial firms. (Two other entities that can run up debt are the government and financial firms.) What appears as a severe recession caused by a banking crisis is, in fact, very largely the outcome of a large increase in household debt that precedes the banking crisis.

The authors make the point that that the recession that happens with a banking crisis that is accompanied by a low level of private debt is not very different from a normal recession. The worst recessions include both high private debt and a banking crisis.

The implication today is that the focus on banks as the source of crises might be misplaced. It is the level of debt in the economy that is the source of the problem; the impact on the banking sector is merely a manifestation of that problem. If we accept this view, it follows that the entire focus on banking reform consequent to the financial crisis is flawed! We should be focusing instead on the level of debt in the economy. We explore this view in Chapter 5.

Banking Crises Are Pervasive and Costly

Banking crises are pervasive, frequent, and impose huge costs on economies. There are numerous studies that document the pervasiveness, frequency, and costs of banking crises. What constitutes a banking crisis?

How do we mark the starting and ending dates of a crisis? How do we estimate the costs of a crisis? Definitions and methodologies vary.

Here, we look at some of the studies that have attempted answers to these questions. Their findings will help us understand just how disruptive banking crises are.

Laeven and Valencia document 147 episodes of banking crises, involving 115 countries, in the period 1970–2011.[6] Clearly, some countries have had multiple crises in the period. The authors define a systemic banking crisis as one that satisfies one or both of the following criteria:

i. There are significant signs of financial distress in the banking system, indicated by bank runs, large bank losses, and bank liquidations.
ii. The government responds to losses in the banking system through significant policy intervention measures.

The first year in which both criteria are met is regarded as the year when the crisis became systemic. Intervention may be regarded as significant if it meets any three of the following criteria:

- Extensive liquidity support (in excess of 5 percent of deposits and liabilities to nonresidents)
- Gross restructuring cost of over 3 percent of GDP (we will elaborate a little later on gross and net restructuring costs)
- Significant bank nationalizations (government takeovers and control of systemically important financial institutions)
- Significant guarantees have been put in place (either full protection of deposits or guarantees of nondeposit liabilities)
- Significant asset repurchases (over 5 percent of GDP)
- Deposit freezes or bank holidays

The authors note that there are instances where governments have intervened on a large scale but without necessarily using three or more of the earlier measures. So they think it a sufficient condition for a crisis to be regarded as systemic if banking system losses exceed 20 percent of loans (or closures of 20 percent of the banking system) or if the fiscal restructuring cost exceeds 5 percent of GDP.

Banking crises entail huge costs for economies. These costs can be measured in several ways:

- The direct fiscal costs of a crisis (i.e., government expenditure incurred on rescuing the banking system)
- The output loss, measured as deviation in GDP from the output trend over a specified period
- The increase in public debt, measured as the increase in public debt over a specified period, starting with the first year of the crisis.

There are many methodological issues involved in each of these ways of measuring the costs of a crisis. The most obvious one is the specification of the period over which the costs are to be measured. Some studies compute the output loss and the increase in debt three years after a crisis; others use a four-year period, including one year prior to the crisis.

These cut-offs are arbitrary for they do not take into account the costs to the economy over a longer period. In conceptual terms, a more precise way would be to compute costs over the entire length of time it takes for the economy to return to the precrisis growth path. The difference between output in the precrisis path and that in the postcrisis path is a measure of the output loss incurred by the economy.

It is also possible (as we shall see a little later) that the economy does not return to the precrisis growth path at all. Then, we will need to take into account the costs to the economy over a much longer period. To the extent that studies do not factor in these considerations and confine their estimate of loss to an arbitrary period, they underestimate the costs to the economy of a banking crisis.

There are issues as well in computing the fiscal costs of a crisis. The direct fiscal cost could vary depending on which items are taken into account: the capital that governments put into banks, the cost of asset purchases, the cost of government guarantees issued during a crisis, and so on. Then again, one could look at the gross fiscal cost, which is the initial outflow that the government faces. Or we could look at the net fiscal cost, which makes adjustments for amounts realized by the government when it sells its stake in banks that are nationalized, the assets it had purchases earlier.

Estimates of Costs of Banking Crises

For the reasons given earlier, there are wide variations in estimates of these costs in a given crisis. One of the best-known studies on banking crises is *This time is different: Eight centuries of financial folly* by the economists Carmen Reinhart and Kenneth Rogoff.[7] For some of the better-known crises in both advanced and emerging economies, Reinhart and Rogoff estimate that the differences in upper and lower bounds of these costs can be anywhere between 0.8 percent of GDP (for the United States) and 51.3 percent of GDP (for Argentina). In other crises, differences in cost estimates of over 10 percentage points are quite common.[8]

Of the measures of the cost of a banking crisis that we cited earlier, the direct fiscal cost of rescuing banks is, perhaps, the least satisfactory. First, it is not a "cost" in economic terms because the cost to the economy in terms of losses in banking has already happened. The fiscal cost merely recognizes these losses.

Second, the actual fiscal cost goes well beyond the costs of bailing out banks. Automatic stabilizers—lower government revenues, an increase in government expenditure—come into play in the depressed conditions created by a banking crisis. As a result, public debt rises. Public debt can rise even further if the government responds with countercyclical measures. The interest cost itself rises as the economy suffers a downgrade. The increase in public debt, is, therefore, a better measure of the cost of a banking crisis than the fiscal cost.

A banking crisis, as Reinhart and Rogoff point out, rarely occurs in isolation. They merely amplify a problem in the economy. Output falls, loans go bad, the supply of credit declines, which leads to a further drop in output and more bad loans. Moreover, banking crises are often accompanied by other crises, including currency crises, debt crises, and inflation crises. It is difficult to say that the costs *associated* with a banking crisis are costs that have occurred *on account* of the crisis. We can only establish correlation, not causality.

Table 1.1 summarizes the costs, as estimated by Laeven and Valencia, whom we cited earlier.

As the table shows, the average output loss was 23 percent of GDP, the increase in public debt was 12.1 percent of GDP and the direct fiscal

Table 1.1 Banking crises outcomes, 1970–2011
(median in percentage of GDP)

Country	Output loss	Increase in debt	Fiscal costs	Peak NPLs in percent of total loans
All	23.0	12.1	6.8	25.0
Advanced	32.9	21.4	3.8	4.0
Emerging	26.0	9.1	10.0	30.0
Developing	1.6	10.9	10.0	37.5

Source: Laeven and Valencia (2012).

cost 6.8 percent of GDP. Output losses and increases in debt tend to be higher in advanced economies. This is understandable. Banking systems in advanced economies are deeper, hence a banking crisis is more disruptive of output. Increases in public debt are larger because the government needs to spend not just to rescue the banking system but because also to stabilize the economy following the disruption of the banking sector.

The costs shown earlier are averages computed across economies. At its most severe, a banking crisis can inflict much larger costs. The authors estimate that, in the 10 costliest banking crises since 1970, the fiscal cost ranged from 31 to 57 percent of GDP; the output loss from 98 to 143 percent of GDP; and the increase in debt from 63 to 108 percent of GDP. In the financial crisis of 2007, the median output loss has been 25 percent of GDP.

Reinhart and Rogoff call banking crises "an equal opportunity menace," that is, they affect advanced and emerging economies almost equally.[9] Until the crisis of 2007, many advanced economies seemed to have graduated out of sovereign debt crises in recent decades after having gone through several episodes of default. The crisis of 2007 showed clearly that this conclusion was misplaced.

Reinhart and Rogoff compute the number of years an economy has spent in a banking crisis. Then, they take into account the number of years since the economy became independent or the number of years since 1800 (if a country became independent before that). Based on these two numbers, they compute the share of years in a banking crisis, that is, how much of its time since independence a country has spent in a banking crisis.[10]

This share turns out to be 7.2 percent for advanced economies and 8.3 percent for emerging economies, about the same. The authors also compute the share of years in a banking crisis since 1945. The figure is 7 percent for advanced economies and 10.8 percent for emerging economies. The United Kingdom, the United States, and France have had 12, 13, and 15 episodes, respectively, of banking crisis since 1800.

Reinhart and Rogoff estimate the impact of a set of particularly severe banking crisis in the post-World War II period. These include what they call the Big Five crises in developed economies (Spain 1977; Norway 1987; Finland 1991; Sweden 1991; and Japan 1992) plus famous episodes in emerging markets: the 1997–98 Asian crises; Columbia 1998; Argentina 2001.[11] They arrive at the following estimates:

- Unemployment rises by an average of 7 percent during the down phase of the cycle, while output declines (from peak to trough) by 9 percent on average.
- Public debt of 86 percent in real terms, relative to precrisis debt, in the three years following a banking crisis.

Honohan and Klingebiel[12] estimate the direct fiscal costs for a sample of 40 countries. They find the average cost to be 12.8 percent of GDP. The cost was even higher in developing countries—14.3 percent. In the early 1908s crises in Argentina and Chile, governments spent 40–55 percent of GDP to clean up financial systems. The costliest crises entailed fiscal costs of upwards of 90 percent of GDP.

The authors mention several factors that lead to underestimation of direct fiscal costs. Costs borne by depositors and other creditors in failed banks are not taken into account. Thanks to bad loans left on the books of banks, spreads widen for other borrowers. There are costs that arise from granting borrowers some monopoly privilege in order to improve profits. Clearly, there is a host of indirect costs that get ignored in the calculations, if only because they are difficult to estimate.

Note that many studies, including the one by Laeven and Valencia, compute the costs of a banking crisis over a limited period. There are studies, however, that show that losses arising from a banking crisis are persistent, that is, the economy does not return to the precrisis path for several years. As a result, studies that focus on losses during a limited period underestimate the costs of banking crises.

For example, one study found that out of 23 countries in the sample, only four reattain their precrisis trend level of output within 17 years after the crisis.[13] The study also found that the average country experiences reduction in current and future output whose discounted present value is between 63 and 302 percent of real GDP in the final precrisis year. This average masks enormous diversity in country experiences—by one measure, nearly a quarter of the countries in the sample exhibit losses of less than four percent of output. Nevertheless, it is worth noting that the cumulative average loss of output is much larger when the full, long-term impact of a banking crisis is taken into account.

The report of the Vickers Commission in the United Kingdom cites a study by the Basel Study on Banking Supervision (BCBS) that corroborates the earlier finding that the costs of a banking crisis are higher than estimated in many studies.[14] The BCBS study estimates the cost of a banking crisis at 19–163 percent of GDP in terms of the net present value of output lost. The median cost turns out to be 63 percent of GDP. The same study estimates that crises occur every 20 to 25 years.

Assuming that a crisis occurs once in 20 years, the annual cost of a banking crisis works out to be 3 percent of GDP. The report concludes that it is worthwhile for governments to incur a cost of up to 3 percent of GDP every year in order to prevent a 5-percent chance of a crisis. We will talk about the Vickers Commission report at greater length in Chapter 4.

The bottom line should be clear enough: Financial crises impose huge costs on economies, so preventing these or finding ways to minimize their impact should be a priority in today's world.

The Subprime Crisis

What is called the "subprime crisis" is a financial crisis that originated in the United States in 2007 and turned into a global crisis from which the world is yet to recover. It was the latest in the episodes of financial crises we have mentioned earlier, and the worst since the Great Depression in the United States of the late-1920s and early 1930s.

The trigger for the subprime crisis was a sudden fall in housing prices in the United States. Housing prices had been rising for several years until 2006. Housing prices peaked in April 2006 after having risen by 15 percent in 2005, the third year of double-digit growth. In 2007, home prices fell by 7 percent. In 2008, they fell by a further 17 percent. By the end of 2009, prices had dropped by 28 percent from the peak of 2006. In some places, the drop was very large: In August 2010, home prices in Las Vegas were 55 percent below their peak of 2006.[15]

The housing bubble, in turn, had been fuelled for years by an expansion in housing loans from banks and other financial institutions. Banks offered loans with very small down payments—as low as 2 or 3 percent in some cases.

They also offered terms that made it easier for borrowers to service the loans in the initial years through low interest rates; in later years, the interest rates would rise. This was done in the belief that housing prices would keep rising and lead to an increase in "home equity," the value of the house that belonged to the borrower. Against this increase in home equity, it was hoped, the borrower could refinance the loan at lower interest rates.

When housing prices collapsed, large numbers of borrowers could not repay their loans and banks suffered huge losses. Delinquencies on mortgages, defined as loans past due for more than 90 days or in foreclosure, had hovered around 1 percent of mortgage loans during the early part of the decade. These rose in 2006 and touched 9.7 percent by the end of 2009.[16]

Financial institutions were exposed to the home market not just through loans. They held large amounts of securities created out of the home loans through a process called "securitization" (we shall talk about this in Chapter 2). These securities are called mortgage-backed securities (MBS) and are rated by the credit rating agencies. As defaults rose on the home loans, the rating agencies downgraded the securities that were derived from these. As a result, the values of the securities fell.

One of the rating agencies, Moody's, began by downgrading some securities in November 2006. Downgrades continued in the months that followed. In July 2007, Moody's downgraded securities, rated Baa, that accounted for 19 percent of all such securities rated in 2006. A few days later, Standard and Poor's, another rating agency, downgraded several of its securities tranches.

By October 2007, Moody's had downgraded and put on watch 13.4 percent of all 2006 subprime MBS it had rated. These now included Aaa securities and Aa securities.[17] The investment banks had created securities packages out of MBS called Collateralized Debt Obligations (CDOs) (these we shall discuss in Chapter 2). CDOs were rated by the rating agencies. Even after it the mass downgrade of MBS in July 2007, Moody's rated 88 percent of the CDOs created thereafter as Aaa.

Apart from banks and investment banks, other financial institutions, such as hedge funds—referred to as "shadow banks"—were heavily exposed to housing loans or MBS. The shadow banks were less rigorously regulated than banks, they held too little capital against the loans they had made and they were heavily dependent on short-term funds.

When the value of MBS declined, investors asked these institutions to put up additional collateral. In order to do so, the shadow banks had to liquidate their securities. This caused market prices to fall even further, which, in turn, led to demands for more collateral. Since banks and investment banks were also exposed to these very securities, they too suffered what is called "contagion" effects.

Against this background, the crisis unfolded with all the relentlessness of a Greek tragedy. By April 2007, several mortgage companies had declared bankruptcy or closed operations. In July 2007, two hedge funds of an investment bank, Bear Stearns, collapsed. In August 2007, the French bank BNP Paribas announced a halt in redemptions in three of its funds. These events gave a further jolt to market confidence.

Bear Stearns itself was heavily exposed to MBS and it had too little capital against its assets—its debt-to-equity ratio in November 2006 was 30:1. This combination, along with its dependence on short-term funds, led to its collapse in March 2008. The Fed arranged a sale of Bear Stearns to J.P. Morgan while providing guarantees worth $29 billion.

The crisis reached its climax in September 2008. On September 7, Fannie Mae and Freddie Mac were to taken into conservatorship by the Federal Housing Finance Agency (FHFA). There followed what has come to be name as the "Lehman weekend at the New York Fed," which was the weekend of September 13–14. Over the weekend, the investment bank Lehman Brothers decided to file for bankruptcy. Another investment bank, Merrill Lynch, was purchased by Bank of America and insurance giant AIG was on the verge of failure.

On September 16, the Fed announced an $85 billion emergency loan to AIG to prevent it from failing. On the same day, the Reserve Primary Fund, a money market mutual fund, saw its net asset value falling below one dollar, which meant that it had lost money. This led to a run on other money market mutual funds. As a result, these funds refused to renew the commercial paper they were funding and switched instead to Treasuries and cash. This led corporations to draw on the lines of credit they had from banks which, in turn, forced banks to pull back from other activities.

Other events followed in quick succession:

- On September 18, the Bush administration announced a Troubled Asset Relief Program (TARP) to recapitalize banks. It was initially rejected by the U.S. Congress. A revised version was passed on October 1.
- On September 21, the Fed agreed to accept Goldman Sachs and Morgan Stanley as bank holding companies which meant that they had access to the central bank as a lender of last resort.
- On September 25, the Federal Deposit Insurance Corporation (FDIC) took Washington Mutual, a bank, into receivership and later sold it to JP Morgan.
- On October 1, Wells Fargo bought Wachovia, another failed bank.

This set of events triggered panic in the financial system and uncertainty in the economy at large. These impacted the funding markets severely. Banks found it difficult to fund themselves in the interbank market; Repo rates shot up; and commercial paper rates also rose sharply following the withdrawal of money market mutual funds from this market.

Several macroeconomic consequences followed. Credit became tighter for both consumers and businesses. The bursting of the housing bubble and the sharp fall in the stock market both contributed to a fall in consumption. As firms and individuals sought to lower their debt by selling

Table 1.2 Economic growth before and after the crisis

GDP growth (annual percent)		
Country group	1996–2006 (Precrisis) Average growth rate	2007–2014 (Postcrisis) Average growth rate
High income	2.78	1.17
Lower middle income	5.69	5.82
Middle income	5.66	5.83
World	3.27	2.17
Low income	4.35	6.16
Low and middle income	5.64	5.84
Upper middle income	5.65	5.84

Source: World Development Indicators, World Bank.

assets or curbing consumption, aggregate demand in the U.S. economy fell. The U.S. economy went into recession and started recovering only in June 2009.

The subprime crisis impacted the rest of the world as well. This happened in various ways. The U.S. recession impacted exports to the United States. Banks in Europe were exposed to subprime assets and they too suffered heavy financial losses. As governments in Europe spent enormous amounts in rescuing banks, the banking crisis morphed into a crisis of sovereign debt. The most striking example was the Greek debt crisis which erupted in May 2010 and is still unresolved. Emerging markets were impacted by the slowdown in the advanced economies and also by reduced inflows of capital or net outflows of capital in the years that followed the crisis.

Global growth has been adversely impacted as a result. Table 1.2 gives the average growth rate for the world economy as well as for high income and developing countries before and after the crisis.

Cost of the Subprime Crisis

Estimating the cost of a crisis, we have seen, depends on several assumptions one makes. First, we need to establish the start date of the crisis. Second, we need to establish the path of real GDP in the absence of a crisis. This would tell us where the GDP would be but for the crisis. Again, the path of the GDP we estimate would depend on how we arrive at the trend rate of growth—whether use the trend rate of, say, the last three years or the trend rate over a longer period in the past. Third, we must determine the end date of the crisis which would be the date on which GDP would return to the precrisis trend path. Here again, estimates of losses would depend on whether the economy's deviation from the precrisis trend path is temporary or permanent. Losses would obviously be greater if the deviation was permanent in nature.

In 2013, the Congressional Budget Office (CBO) estimated the cumulative loss of output arising from the financial crisis of 2007–09 assuming that the U.S. economy would resume the precrisis trend path in 2018. It arrived at an estimate of $5.3 trillion in lost output.[18] The IMF estimated the cumulative percentage difference between actual and trend real GDP for the four years following the start of banking crises in various countries. They found a loss of 31 percent of GDP for the 2007–09 crisis in the United States.[19]

Note that both the studies cited earlier assume that the loss of output is confined to a certain period. The CBO study notes that if one assumes that losses are permanent in nature, the estimate could be above 100 percent of GDP or $13 trillion.

Output losses are one measure of the cost of a financial crisis. There are other measures we can look at. One is the impact on unemployment. The CBO noted that the monthly unemployment rate had peaked at around 10 percent in October 2009 and remained above 8 percent for over three years, making it the "longest stretch of unemployment above 8 percent in the United States since the Great Depression."[20] The median household net worth fell by nearly $49,100 per family or by nearly 39 percent between 2007 and 2010. This was the result of the decline in home prices and values of stocks and bonds.

Another measure of the cost of a crisis, as we have noted earlier, is the rise in public debt. Between the end of 2007 and the end of 2010, public debt of the federal government in the United States rose from 36 percent of GDP to 62 percent.[21]

Laurence Ball has estimated the impact of the crisis on the OECD economies. He does so by taking the path that output was following before the financial crisis (using OECD estimates before 2007) and extrapolating this through 2015.[22] He compares the precrisis trend to estimates of potential output made by OECD in May 2014. He ascribes the difference to the effects of the recession. To check for robustness, he carries out a similar exercise using IMF data from October 2007 and April 2014. His key results are shown in Table 1.3.

Table 1.3 Losses in OECD countries following subprime crisis

Country	Loss in potential, 2015	Output gap, 2015	Growth rate of potential, precrisis	Growth of potential, 2014–15
Australia	1.83	2.27	3.33	3.11
Austria	7.14	2.64	2.36	1.75
Belgium	8.82	1.19	2.07	1.36
Canada	9.71	−0.16	2.9	2.08
Czech Republic	22.4	3.52	4.62	1.92
Denmark	11.32	1.63	1.76	0.86
Finland	18.99	3.08	3.09	1.04
France	8.58	3.08	2.08	1.48
Germany	3.39	−0.87	1.52	1.25
Greece	35.4	7.59	3.96	−0.15
Hungary	30.51	0.69	4.42	0.98
Ireland	34.15	4.45	5.75	0.93
Italy	12.05	3.74	1.34	0.11
Japan	9.57	−0.89	1.4	0.79
Netherlands	8.53	4.09	2.14	1.2
New Zealand	7.47	−1.22	3.07	2.53
Poland	7.42	0.16	4.11	2.91
Portugal	13.74	4.98	1.83	0.49
Spain	22.33	3.52	3.47	0.83
Sweden	8.66	0.76	3.02	2.41
Switzerland	−0.88	0.39	1.81	2.04
United Kingdom	12.37	0.32	2.66	1.85
United States	5.33	1.87	2.57	2.23
Weighted Average	8.38	1.49	2.39	1.68

Source: Laurence M. Ball (2014).

The first column in Table 1.3 gives the loss of potential output. The second gives the deviation of actual from the potential output. The two together give the total loss of output in 2015. The average loss in potential output for 23 economies, weighted by the sizes of their economies, was 8.4 percent for 2015. For the United States, the loss of potential, going by OECD forecasts, was 5.3 percent in 2015. (Going by IMF forecasts, the loss was 7.7 percent in 2015, which is broadly consistent with Ball's estimates.)

In many countries, the deviation of potential output from the pre-crisis path was smaller than the deviation of actual output from the same path but only by modest amounts. In 2015, for the OECD economies as a whole, the average deviation of actual output from potential output was 9.87 percent, which was split into 8.38 percent loss in output potential and 1.39 percent gap between potential and actual output. This suggests a strong "hysteresis" effect, meaning that as the actual output departed from the trend, so did the potential output.

In many countries, the growth *rate* of potential was also impacted, not just the potential output. This is shown in Columns 3 and 4 in Table 1.3. We can see that in many countries, the growth *rate* was impacted adversely, not just the potential output. The countries that had the largest current loss in potential output also had bad prospects going forward. This meant that the losses of potential output with respect to the precrisis trend would grow over time.

Putting together the loss of potential output and a slower growth rate, Ball's study also suggests that the loss of output from a financial crisis is much greater than that estimated by studies that focus on a limited period around a crisis.

We do not have estimates of the loss of output in emerging markets as these were impacted by the global crisis with a lag of several years. However, the estimates of the loss of output in the United States and the OECD that we have cited earlier should make it clear that the financial crisis of 2007 has had a lasting impact on global economic output.

Why do severe recessions such as that of 2007 have a lasting impact? Why do economies take so long to recover? Several explanations have been put forward:

- Capital accumulation falls during recession.
- Long-term employment is adversely impacted as several workers lose their skills due to prolonged unemployment.
- Growth of total factor productivity goes down perhaps because of underinvestment in new technologies.

We need to fear banking crises precisely because their effects are long lasting.

Summary

Banks are fragile entities that are prone to failure. This is because they operate at high levels of leverage and they use short-term borrowings to fund loans of longer maturity. Bank failure has serious externalities: The costs to the economy are greater than the private costs. In order to prevent banks from failing, we have various regulations in place. These include: licensing of banks, deposit insurance, and lender of last resort facilities provided by the central bank.

These measures, however, have proved inadequate to deal with the bank failure. This is especially true of the too-big-to-fail problem, the fact that banks that are very large simply cannot be allowed to fail and, therefore, have incentives to take excessive risks.

It is not clear whether an economic contraction causes a banking crisis or a banking crisis causes an economic contraction. We do know, however, that the two are correlated. Moreover, problems in the banking sector do exacerbate problems in the economy. One theory put forward recently is that banking crises have to do with a large buildup of private debt, they have less to do with banks *per se*.

Banking crises impose large costs on the economy. These costs have been estimated using various methodologies. There is evidence that the effects of banking crises are large and persistent.

The subprime crisis, as the financial crisis of 2007 and thereafter is often called, arose from a fall in housing prices and the exposure of financial institutions to housing assets in one form or another. It resulted in the failure of several financial institutions and the rescue of others. The costs to the world economy have been large and the world economy is yet to recover from the impact of the crisis.

CHAPTER 2

Causes of the Subprime Crisis

America's housing market had seen a rise in prices for several years until 2006. Thereafter, the bubble burst. Banks and other financial institutions that were heavily exposed to the housing market began to fail as a result, dragging the U.S. economy into a recession. As we noted in Chapter 1, two hedge funds promoted by an investment bank, Bear Stearns, failed in July 2007, an episode that can be said to mark the start of the financial crisis of 2007.

A collapse in housing prices has happened in several economies in the past, notably in Japan in the 1990s. The United States and other economies have been through many recessions before. What is striking about the financial crisis of 2007 in the United States is its sheer severity—it has stretched out for several years now and it has had a global impact. The financial crisis has come to be regarded as the biggest crisis in the United States since the Great Crash of 1929. The recession that followed and impacted the global economy is characterized as the Great Recession.

How do we explain the financial crisis of 2007 and the Great Recession that followed? One approach that is common is to ascribe the crisis to a large number of factors. This has come to be known as the "Murder-on-the-Orient-Express" theory of the crisis. Some of you may have read Agatha Christie's novel of that name or seen the popular movie that came out of it. In the novel, one character gets murdered while taking a trip on the Orient Express, a train that ran from Istanbul to Paris over several days. Twelve stab wounds are found on him.

The detective Hercule Poirot investigates the murder and solves it before the train reaches its destination: The murder was committed, not by 1 individual, but 12 individuals, each of whom had reason to loathe the murdered man. There were thus 12 villains in the picture. We can similarly identify 12 villains widely believed to have caused the financial crisis of 2007. These are:

    i. A housing bubble in the United States and elsewhere
    ii. Political pressure in the United States to expand the supply of home loans
    iii. Global macroeconomic imbalances
    iv. Loose monetary policies
    v. Excessive financialization
    vi. Belief in market efficiency
    vii. Fannie Mae and Freddie Mac, two government-sponsored entities
    viii. Greedy and incompetent bankers and financiers
    ix. Basel rules
    x. Credit rating agencies
    xi. Greedy consumers
    xii. Regulatory failure

In what follows, we will take a close look at each of these villains, one by one. We will then make it clear that we do not subscribe to the Murder-on-the-Orient-Express theory. We will argue that one particular villain stands out. For our analysis, we draw extensively on the report of the Financial Crisis Inquiry Commission (FCIC) set up by the U.S. government to investigate the causes of the crisis.

A Housing Bubble in the United States and Elsewhere

As we outlined in Chapter 1, there is little doubt that the global crisis of 2007 had its roots in a housing crisis. Housing prices shot up in the United States and elsewhere over 1997 to 2006. Thereafter, prices collapsed. There is, however, no consensus on what caused the bubble.

Large numbers of people had bought houses with the help of mortgages. It turned out that many did not have the income to service their mortgages. They had been provided mortgages in the belief that home prices would keep rising and they would be able to refinance their mortgages at lower interest rates out of the increase in prices. Rising prices were thus crucial to their ability to service their mortgages. When housing prices collapsed, borrowers could no longer service their mortgages. Banks and other lenders faced huge losses and borrowers faced foreclosures of their homes.

There was a housing bubble not only in the United States but in Europe and elsewhere. In the United States, home prices increased by 87 percent in real terms between 1997 and 2006. Thereafter, prices dropped sharply.[1] The increase in home prices was out of line with increases in other relevant variables such as building costs, population growth, and interest rates. The increase in home prices took place across cities in the United States, across price tiers (low-priced, medium-priced, and high-priced homes) and across countries.

What explains this bubble? Yale economist Robert Shiller ascribes it to what he calls a "social contagion of boom thinking," that is, a situation where people everywhere come to believe that prices will keep rising.[2] People see prices rising, they hear other people say that prices will keep rising and then most people simply come to believe it. Some sort of herd mentality is at work. The media plays a role in fostering these beliefs by carrying "new era" stories, that is, stories about a new era of faster economic growth having dawned. Price increases generate optimism which causes more spending, which causes more price increases and so on.

Shiller argues that other factors blamed for the crisis, which we will soon look at, such as low interest rates, weak underwriting standards for loans, and the failure of regulators to rein in aggressive lending were all products of the bubble psychology—all the players concerned believed that home prices would continue to rise. It was the psychology that was the key to rising home prices.

One view that especially gained acceptance was that more rapid economic growth in China, India, Brazil, and Russia would create a new class of wealthy people who would bid up the price of real estate and other assets. This, perhaps, explains why the housing bubble of the 2000s was not a local phenomenon but a widespread one and why prices of assets other than real estate also rose in the period. In short, on this view, the housing bubble was the result of what economists call "animal spirits" among economic agents, large numbers of people thinking that things will get better and better. We shall examine this view critically a little later.

Political Pressure in the United States to Expand the Supply of Home Loans

American politicians have long sought to widen home ownership. In the years preceding the crisis, politicians in the United States came to view home ownership as something of an antidote to widening inequality. To this end, they encouraged measures that promoted house loans, such as tax deductibility of interest on these loans, and allowed regulators to lower standards for housing loans.

Inequality in the United States has widened in recent decades. In 1975, those in the 90th percentile in terms of income earned three times more than those in the 10th percentile. In 2005, the former earned five times the latter. Similarly, the differential between those in the 90th percentile and those in the middle—the 50th percentile—has widened.[3]

Inequality has both political and economic consequences. It leads to greater social unrest. It also impacts adversely on economic growth: Since the rich consume less at the margin than the poor, consumption growth cannot be sustained without addressing income inequality.

Correcting inequality would require measures such as massive investment in higher education, making education more accessible, addressing problems in communities and families, progressive taxation and income redistribution. Raghuram Rajan, professor at Chicago's Booth School of Business, has argued that, instead of making the effort required for these measures, politicians found it simpler to try and widen home ownership. They tweaked regulations relating to banks to enable home ownership to spread.[4] Rising home prices give owners a sense that their overall incomes are rising even when wages are stagnant.

America has a long history of measures aimed at increasing home ownership.[5] Following the Depression, during which several home owners defaulted on their mortgages (which were typically for 5 years then), the government created two agencies, the Home Owner's Loan Corporation (HOLC) and the Federal Housing Authority (FHA). The HOLC was intended to buy defaulted mortgages from banks and thrifts and restructure them into 20-year fully amortizing mortgages. This made it easier for home owners to service mortgages.

However, the government did not want to hold on to the mortgages forever through HOLC. It wanted to be able to sell these to private parties. This would be possible only if private parties, which had long been averse to holding long-term loans, could be persuaded that there was no default risk on these mortgages. The way out was to create the FHA which would provide insurance for mortgages for a fee. The FHA set strict limits on the maximum loan it would finance (as a percentage of the value of the property) and the amount of the loan it would insure.

HOLC was wound up in 1936. In its place came the Federal National Mortgage Association (FNMA or Fannie Mae). Fannie Mae bought FHA-insured mortgages and financed itself through long-term bonds issued to investors, such as pension funds and insurance companies, with long-term horizons. Thus, banks, while originating loans, did not have to bear the interest-rate risk involved in holding long-term mortgages financed by short-term deposits. They were essentially distributors of loans that would rest on the books of Fannie Mae.

In 1968, Fannie Mae was split into two: Government National Mortgage Association (GNMA or Ginnie Mae), which guarantees securities backed by mortgages issued by government agencies, including the FHA; and a new, privatized Fannie Mae which continued to purchase mortgages from banks. Soon after, in order to create competition for Fannie Mae, the government created Freddie Mac (Federal Home Loan Mortgage Corporation) as a private corporation. It has essentially the same charter as Fannie Mae. The two agencies came to be known as Government-Sponsored Enterprises (GSEs).

Both Fannie Mae and Freddie Mac buy mortgages from lenders and either hold these mortgages in their portfolios or package them into securities and sell them to other investors. In the years before the crisis, the two agencies also got into the business of buying mortgage-backed securities from others. The two agencies, while owned by private shareholders, were exempted from state and local taxes, had government appointees on their boards and had a line of credit from the U.S. Treasury.

In the years that followed, governments used the two agencies to promote home ownership. In 1992, the U.S. Congress enacted the GSE Act. The Act was intended to give low and moderate income borrowers better access to credit through the two GSEs. It sought to do so by stipulating that a certain percentage of mortgage purchases—30 percent—made by Fannie Mae and Freddie Mac should be from these categories. This was a radical departure from the original mission of the two agencies. This target was increased to 42 percent in 1995.[6] We elaborate on the role played by Fannie Mae and Freddie Mac a little later.

These efforts received a new impetus during the terms of Presidents Bill Clinton and George Bush. In 1995, Clinton declared that he wanted to boost home ownership from 65.1 to 67.5 percent of families by 2000.[7] Under Clinton, the Housing and Urban Development (HUD) department increased the funding target for low-income housing for the two agencies—from 42 percent in 1995 to 50 percent in 2000.[8] By 2008, the figure had risen to 56 percent.[9]

The Community Reinvestment Act (CRA) of 1977 mandated banks to lend more in their local markets, especially in low-income areas. In 1995, President Bill Clinton loosened housing rules by rewriting the CRA. Earlier, banks were merely required to show that they were making efforts to reach out to low-income borrowers. Now, they were required to show that they were actually making loans to such borrowers. The Clinton administration also pushed regulators to enforce CRA more vigorously by holding out threats of fines to banks that did not comply adequately.

One contention that has emerged following the subprime crisis is that the focus on CRA was a significant factor contributing to the crisis as it put banks on the same footing as the two GSEs and the FHA in seeking out low-income borrowers. However, the FCIC did not believe this to be true. Only 6 percent of high-cost loans, which are a proxy for subprime loans, had any relation to the CRA. The FCIC also found that loans made by CRA-regulated lenders in their neighborhoods were half as likely to default as similar loans made by mortgage lenders not subject to the law.[10]

A third initiative toward greater home ownership was the "Best Practices Initiative" launched by the HUD in 1994 to which 117 members of the Mortgage Bankers Association eventually adhered. This was intended to explicitly lower underwriting standards in order to promote access to credit of low income borrowers.[11] Politicians' push for greater home ownership, it is argued, resulted in underwriting standards being lowered by regulators and banks alike, led to loans being made to large numbers of people who were not creditworthy and created a housing bubble, the bursting of which brought the financial crisis.

American politicians' enthusiasm for pushing home mortgages remains strong even after the crisis. In October 2014, the head of Federal Housing Finance Authority announced plans to reintroduce mortgages through Freddie Mac and Fannie Mae with deposits as low as 3 percent. This went against the recommendation of a consortium of federal agencies in 2011 that mortgage-backed securities should only include mortgages with a minimum deposit of 20 percent.[12]

Subprime lending was rare or nonexistent outside the United States. Subprime lending was 8 percent of all mortgages in the United Kingdom, 5 percent in Canada, 2 percent in Australia, and negligible elsewhere.[13] In the United States, subprime mortgages accounted for 23.5 percent of all mortgages in 2006.[14] Half the mortgage loans outstanding the United States by the middle of 2007 were subprime or alt-A mortgages, that is, mortgages of relatively lower quality.[15]

The FHA, created under the National Housing Act of 1934, sets standards for construction and underwriting and insures loans made by banks and other private lenders for home building. An FHA loan is a mortgage insured by the FHA. Borrowers with an FHA loan pay for mortgage insurance and this is supposed to protect lenders from default.

An FHA program in 1999 gives us an idea of how generous the FHA's terms for insuring mortgages were.[16] The down payment required was only 1.25 to 3 percent of the sale price and significantly lower than the minimum required by lenders for conventional or subprime loans. Moreover, an FHA loan could be structured so that borrowers did not have to pay more than 3 percent of the total out-of-pocket funds, including down payment. FHA focused only on the last 12 to 24 month credit history, did not insist on a minimum credit score and its insurance was available to people with no established credit.

The record we have outlined previously speaks for itself. Political pressure to spread home ownership and the use of government agencies for the purpose led to large amounts of credit being made available to those who were not in a position to service it. It was thus an important factor contributing to the crisis.

Global Macroeconomic Imbalances

For several years preceding the crisis, the global economy was characterized by large macroeconomic imbalances. China, Japan, oil-producing countries, and some East Asian economies were running up large current account surpluses. The United States, the United Kingdom, Spain, Ireland, and other countries were having large current account deficits. Since the obverse of a current deficit is a capital account inflow, large amounts of capital were flowing to the latter economies.

In effect, the argument goes, the surplus savings of countries with current account surpluses was being directed into economies with a current account (and hence a savings) deficit. The effect of these inflows of capital was to drive interest rates low and to encourage borrowing and consumption in economies with current account deficits.

This has come to be characterized as the "savings glut" argument, that is, that there were excess savings in some parts of the world economy and these were routed to parts that were deficient in savings. Savers in China and elsewhere were willing to finance the excess consumption of American households. So, in a way, the savers are as culpable as the borrowers.

This thesis seems persuasive and has come to be widely accepted. On close examination, however, it has several flaws. First, it assumes that that a current account surplus is the *result* of a decision on the part of households in some countries to save more than they invest. This need not be the case. An economy's exports could be competitive and, as a result, they would generate profits for producers. This leads to higher investment, which translates into higher income and hence higher savings. Thus, savings can be the consequence of a current account surplus rather than *vice versa*.[17]

Second, it is not as if an economy needed to have a current account surplus with the United States in order for investors in that economy to invest in the U.S. securities. As economist Barry Eichengreen points out, it was perfectly possible for foreign investors to buy the U.S. mortgage-related securities without their economies running up a current account surplus with the United States—Europe did not have a current account surplus with the United States and yet European banks held large amounts of the U.S. credit products. He also points out that barely a third of

America's gross external liabilities in 2002–2007 can be explained by the country's cumulative current account deficits.

Third, the impact of capital inflows into the United States on interest rates was also not as great as is made out to be. According to some estimates, the impact was 45 to 90 basis points. It is hard to believe that there would have been no financial crisis if only the U.S. interest rates had been higher by 90 basis points.[18]

Loose Monetary Policy in the United States

Consequent to the dotcom bubble in the United States in 2001, the Federal Reserve Board cut interest rates. The real Fed funds rate was negative for 31 months from October 2002 to April 2005.[19] It is argued that the Fed kept its rates low for too long. It could afford to do so as there was foreign capital waiting to flow into the U.S. securities, thanks to global macroeconomic imbalances. Cheap credit helped fuel the boom in housing prices. Even when it was evident that a housing bubble was in the making, the Fed did not think it necessary to change its monetary stance.

There are reasons for doubting this thesis. Shiller points out that the period of the housing boom was three times as long as the period of low interest rates.[20] Moreover, the housing boom was accelerating at a time when the United States increased interest rates in 1999. Were the U.S. interest rates too low in 2003–2004? According to some, it was 300 basis points below where it should have been, going by the well-known Taylor Rule in macroeconomics. The Fed, they argued, should have tightened interest rates. This would have increased savings, reduced America's current account deficit and prevented the asset bubble in housing to get out of hand.

Plausible as this sounds, we need to ask how exactly low short-term interest rates impact the housing market which is based on long-term funds.[21] Assuming that the short-term policy rate is too low, it does not follow that rates on 30-year housing mortgages should also be too low. Eichengreen points out that policy rates influence the housing market through adjustable-rate mortgages (ARMs), that is, mortgages on which interest rates rise over time.

When ARM rates are low, home buyers are lured into the market. Did the ARM rates fall sharply in response to low policy rates? One way to answer this question is to look at the gap between ARM rates and rates on conventional 30-year mortgages. While this gap rose, former Fed Chairman Ben Bernanke has pointed out that the gap was never very large. Second, ARM originations peaked two years before the housing market, so the connection between ARM rates and the housing bubble does not appear very strong. One of the main reasons the housing bubble happened is that credit spreads—the difference between risk-free rates and rates on risky assets fell sharply. Loose monetary policy—or low policy rates—cannot explain the fall in credit spreads.

In general, we cannot assume that low interest rates automatically trigger a housing bubble. There have been economies, such as Japan, that had interest rates close to zero without a housing bubble building up. Moreover, housing prices have collapsed elsewhere without causing a national economic crisis, much less an international one. Loose monetary policy may have amplified the housing bubble in the United States but it is hard to argue that it caused the bubble in the first place.

Excessive Financialization

It is well understood that the growth of the financial sector is important for economic development. Financial sector growth is seen to facilitate economic growth. It appears, however, that there is an optimal level beyond which the growth of the financial sector is harmful to the economy because it renders the financial sector vulnerable to collapse. There is such a thing as excessive "financialization" of the economy, that is, growth in the financial sector that is unrelated to the needs of the real economy.

How do we measure financialization? Several measures have been proposed in the literature: the ratio of private credit to GDP; the share of the financial sector in GDP; volume of trading of stocks, bonds, derivatives, and foreign exchange trading in relation to GDP; and so on. By each of these measures, financialization soared in the run-up to the financial crisis.

Adair Turner, a former chairman of the Financial Services Authority in the United Kingdom, has written a fascinating book on what went wrong with modern finance. He provides data to show how the financial sector has got swollen over the years.[22] In the United Kingdom, finance grew by 4.4 percent per year in the period 1856 to 2008 while the economy grew at 2.1 percent. In the United States, between 1850 and the crash of 1929, finance's share of national income grew from 2 to 6 percent. Thereafter, the share of finance fell and in 1970 it stood at 4 percent. From 1970 to 2008, the share of finance more than doubled.

Table 2.1 provides data on one commonly used measure for financial penetration, the credit to GDP ratio for select economies. We can see that, except in Germany and Japan, credit expanded in these economies. The expansion was large in both the United States and the United Kingdom.

Table 2.2 provides data on another measure of financial development, the ratio of market capitalization to GDP. Again, this gives us an idea of the expansion of the financial sector in select economies.

The financial sector exists in order to lubricate the wheels of the real economy. One would expect, therefore, that financial sector assets and

Table 2.1 Credit to GDP ratio for select countries (percent)

Country	1996	2006
Australia	71.5	113.8
Brazil	40.8	35.4
China	89.8	110.0
United Kingdom	108.9	161.3
India	23.0	43.2
Japan	202.4	190.5
Russian Federation	8.3	30.9
United States	137.2	197.7
Germany	103.5	101.7

Source: World Bank, World Development Indicators.

Table 2.2 Market capitalization of listed domestic companies (% of GDP)

Country	1996	2006
Australia	77.9	146.7
United Kingdom	130.9	146.1
Japan	64.2	105.9
United States	104.7	141.2
Germany	26.6	54.5

Source: World Bank, World Development Indicators.

liabilities would grow in line with nonfinancial sector assets and liabilities. We find instead that financial sector assets and liabilities grew a great deal more, so that much of the lending was within the financial sector itself.

Some of this was reflected in the volumes of securities traded in relation to the underlying physical good. The value of oil futures has risen from less than 10 percent of physical oil production and consumption in 1984 to more than 10 times that of oil production and consumption. Global foreign exchange trading is now around 73 times global trade in goods and services. The notional value of outstanding interesting rate derivatives had soared from zero in 1980 to more than \$400 trillion by 2007.[23]

These are all separate indicators of financial development. Many researchers have relied on measures that focused on the banking sector alone. These measures can be misleading. For instance, bank credit as a percentage of GDP in the United States has been largely stable in the period 1980 to 2013. However, the assets of the nonbanking sector have more than doubled. To get around this problem, the IMF has developed a comprehensive measure of financial development (FD index).[24]

The FD index includes financial institutions as well as markets and measures the growth of both on three indicators: depth, access, and efficiency. Thus, we have a total of six indicators. Each of these indicators is normalized on a score of 0 to 1. An aggregate score is then arrived at by assigning suitable weights to each indicator.

Based on a sample of 128 countries, the IMF found a bell-shaped relationship between financial development and growth in the period 1980–2013. Financial development increases growth but, at higher levels of financial development, growth weakens and even becomes negative. The positive effects begin to decline when the index is in the range of 0.4–0.7.

Beyond 0.7, the effects tend to become negative. One reason could be that too much finance renders an economy more prone to booms and busts. Another could be that the financial sector tends to lead to a diversion of human capital away from more productive sectors. The United States had an index of around 0.8, which points to an overdeveloped financial sector. It does appear that, in many countries, the financial sector has grown too big for the good of the economy.

Belief in Market Efficiency

There was a widespread belief in the years leading up to the crisis that markets are efficient. Market efficiency means that all available information is factored into prices of securities. From this proposition, several inferences have been drawn. One, efficient markets are also rational and hence the prices at any given point in time are the correct prices. Two, market discipline will prevent excessive risk-taking. Three, financial innovation is beneficial; if it were not, efficient markets would weed out such innovation.[25]

Every one of these inferences has turned out to be incorrect. Efficient markets are not always rational. Prices do depart from rational levels because of herd behavior in the markets—for instance, in times of optimism, everybody starts buying stocks in the expectation that prices will keep rising.

Similarly, it is incorrect to suppose that market discipline will prevent excessive risk-taking and the bank failures that follow. The Basel norms that govern banks worldwide (about which more a little later) see market discipline as an important pillar of bank regulation. With the benefit of bitter experience, we know now that in the years leading to the crisis of 2007, the markets failed to impose the necessary discipline on banks. As a result, many failed.

Bank share prices, for instance, did not capture the risks that these banks were exposed to. Market pressures to increase return on capital caused banks to hold less capital, rather than more. The banking system was left with too little capital in the face of losses. This is a clear instance of the market being not so efficient.

Let us take another case of market failure. Credit default swaps (CDS) are instruments designed to give protection against default to credits. If the risk of default is high, then the CDS "spread," the insurance premium that the buyer of the CDS pays for protection against default, is supposed to capture default risk and create the necessary discipline in various market players. If the spread is very large, investors know that the risk of default is high and steer clear of the underlying credit. However, again in the run-up to the 2007 crisis, CDS prices did not adequately capture the risks involved. Low CDS spreads lured investors into taking credit risks that turned out to be higher than the spreads indicated.

Similarly, as we shall see later, the securitization of housing loans—housing loans getting converted these into tradable securities and being sold to investors—added to risks in the system by creating incentives for originators to lower underwriting standards for these loans. The markets failed to exercise the necessary checks on securitization by not pricing securitized products correctly. These examples show that it is simply not true that efficient markets will constrain excessive risk-taking.

Finally, it's worth noting that innovations are not beneficial to the same extent. Financial innovation does not have the same benefits as innovation in the goods sector and, indeed, can be harmful. Innovation in the goods sector is about technological advances and increased productivity in the economy and it results in rents or superior gains to the innovator.

In the financial sector, gains from innovation often relate to superior information about prices, not with technological advance. Efficiency in the market is about the information becoming widely available so that abnormal gains from superior price information disappear. However, such efficiency has to do entirely with existing resources or assets; it does lead to any increase in productivity in the economy.

On the contrary, we know that financial innovation has the potential to do harm. For instance, the important innovation we mentioned previously, CDS, was used not just to hedge a risk in an underlying security held by an investor; it was used for the purpose of pure speculation. As a result, the value of CDS issued rose out of all proportion to the underlying security. When default happened on the underlying securities, the issuers of CDS were unable to honor their commitments.

More generally, financial innovation has contributed to the increase in financialization mentioned earlier, that is, a disproportionate increase in size of the financial sector relative to the real economy. This benefits the financial sector and those involved in it. However, it does not benefit the economies involved. On the contrary, a swollen financial sector leads to increased risk for economies.

Fannie Mae and Freddie Mac

We referred earlier to two GSEs, Fannie Mae and Freddie Mac, that were intended to promote home ownership. The two GSEs, we noted, were in the business of buying mortgages from banks, securitizing some of these mortgages and also buying securitized mortgages from others.

There was a basic flaw in the business model of the two GSEs. They were privately owned. However, because they had a public mission (the spread of home ownership), their debt carried an implicit government guarantee. This amounted to a subsidy from the government because it lowered the cost of borrowing of the GSEs. The greater the debt carried by them, the greater was the value of the subsidies or the safety net. This created three different problems and increased risk in the financial system.

First, shareholders and managers at the GSEs were rewarded for having as little equity capital as they could and for carrying large amounts of debt instead. Holders of debt did not insist on shareholders putting more equity into banks and GSEs because they knew they were protected by the government.

Under regulatory norms for banks, known as Basel II, banks were required to hold only $4 in capital toward $100 of mortgage loans. The GSEs were required to hold even less capital against mortgage loans—$2.50. For the mortgage-backed securities they sold to others, the GSEs were required to hold a mere 45 cents for every $100 of mortgages sold. As a result, the combined leverage ratio of the two GSEs—that is, the ratio of debt to equity—including loans they held and guaranteed, was 74:1 by the end of 2007.[26]

Second, buyers of these mortgage-backed securities, in turn, knew that the GSEs and the banks that sold these guaranteed buyers against default on these securities. Hence, the buyers had every incentive for buying securitized portfolios of mortgages from GSEs and banks.

Moreover, precisely because of the guarantee offered by the sellers, banks needed to hold only $1.60 in capital against every $100 invested in such securities that were AAA-rated (compared to the $4 they had to hold as capital if they made mortgage loans themselves). Thus, if a bank sold a $100 mortgage to a GSE and bought it back as a mortgage-backed security (MBS), the total capital in the system against the two transactions together was $2.05 (45 cents to be held by GSEs plus $1.60 to be held by banks). This is called "regulatory arbitrage."[27]

Securitization on the part of the GSEs created a third problem: It contributed to the expansion of risky mortgage finance. Securitization increased the amount of mortgage finance available. The GSEs would buy mortgages from the banks, thus making finance available for more mortgages; the GSEs would then securitize these mortgages and sell them to investors, so that the GSEs, in turn, could buy more mortgages from the banks. Once the supply of finance increased, GSEs lowered the standards they had for buying mortgages from banks. Banks (and financial institutions), in turn, strove to push mortgages onto larger numbers of people by lowering their own standards for making loans.

GSEs also contributed to greater finance being available by becoming big purchasers of non-GSE securities from the market. Their share of non-GSE securities increased from 10.5 percent in 2002 to 40 percent in 2004 before falling to 28 percent in 2008.[28]

Overall, however, GSEs were less at fault in respect of lending standards than the banks. During the crisis, GSE securities maintained their value and did not inflict significant losses on those who had purchased these. At the end of 2008, the delinquency rate on loans purchased or guaranteed by the GSEs was 6.2 percent compared to 28.3 percent for other financial firms.[29] The FCIC concludes that the GSEs "contributed to the crisis, but were not a primary cause."

So, yes, politicians did use GSEs to spread home ownership has some merit but the damage done on this account was less than that of other factors.

Greedy and Incompetent Bankers and Financiers

When banks fail, the costs are often borne not by the debt holder but by the tax payer. The government intervenes to recapitalize failed banks. This happens because, as we explained in Chapter 1, bank failures can impose significant costs on the economy. The state would like to avoid these costs. Knowing that they will be bailed out by the state, debt holders do not impose discipline on shareholders and managers.

In such a situation, bankers will seek to maximize profits using five strategies. Andrew Haldane, a former Executive Director of the Bank of England, tells us what these strategies are:[30]

- Higher leverage: As a bank's leverage rises, so does its return on equity (RoE). But higher leverage also increases the bank's risk. As shareholders and managers know that the costs of failure are ultimately borne by tax payers, there is every incentive for them to take risky gambles. If the gambles pay off, shareholders and managers benefit. If they do not, it is debt holders who bear the losses. "Heads-I-win-tails-you-lose" sums up the attitude of shareholders and managers. This is precisely what happened in the run-up to the banking crisis. There was a trend toward higher leverage.

- Higher trading assets: Banks can also take advantage of leverage to boost profit by increasing the proportion of trading assets. These assets are marked to market. In a rising market, therefore, trading assets deliver capital gains.

- Greater diversification: Diversification is said to lower non-systematic or idiosyncratic risk at the firm level. However, by leading to similarity in asset portfolios of banks, it can increase the risk of the system as a whole.

- High default assets: American banks were constrained in the use of leverage by a leverage ratio prescribed by regulators. (This is the accounting ratio of equity to total assets.) They responded to this constraint by simply taking on riskier assets, such as subprime loans and exotic securities. The incentive was the same as in increased leverage. If the riskier assets yielded high payoffs, bankers stood to benefit; if they did not, the tax payer would foot the bill.

- Out-of-the-money options: Another way to take high risks is to write deep out-of-the-money options, such as selling protection in the CDS market. In good states of the world, the writer earns a steady fee. In bad states, there is a huge loss.

Bankers had incentives to take such risks because their rewards were linked to RoE. Higher the RoE, higher the reward for bankers. In 1989, the CEOs of the seven largest banks in the world earned an average of $2.8 million. By 2007, CEO compensation among the largest U.S. banks had risen to $26 million. Haldane estimates that had CEO compensation been indexed to RoE in 1989, it would have risen to just that much in 2007!

The incentives for investment bankers were similar and so were the actions of investment bankers. True, investment banks were not (until the crisis) subject to bailout by the government and it was up to the lenders to investment banks to have exercised discipline. They could not do so because the riskiness of securities held by investment banks was not clear to them—these securities enjoyed high ratings from the rating agencies.

In the financial system, higher risk-taking took the form of greater exposure to lower quality loans. The volume of subprime and nontraditional loans rose sharply. In 2000, the top 25 nonprime lenders originated $105 billion in loans; this figure rose to $188 billion in 2002 and $310 billion in 2003. Nonprime lending surged to $730 billion in 2004 and $1 trillion in 2005.[31] Independent consumer finance companies emerged for making subprime loans.

Banks were quick to sense the potential of subprime lending and set up subsidiaries for the purpose (e.g., CitiFinancial). The finance companies funded themselves with short-term lines of credit from commercial and investment banks. They did not always keep the loans themselves. They sold the loans to banks which securitized these loans and sold them to others or kept these themselves.

In 2000, Citigroup acquired Associates First Capital, the second biggest subprime lender. Soon, there were three types of players in subprime origination and securitization: banks and thrifts, investment banks, and nonbank mortgage lenders.[32] Investment banks found that banks had developed the expertise to securitize and distribute loans on their own. So the investment banks moved into mortgage origination so that they could have access to loans to securitize.

Lehman Brothers, Bear Stearns, and Merrill Lynch all acquired subprime originators. Two types of models emerged: originate-to-hold and originate-to-distribute. In the former, the originators held the securitized assets to maturity. There was an incentive, therefore, to ensure quality of the loans acquired. In the latter, mortgages were to be passed on to others, so the originator merely faced reputation risks.

Lenders knew that borrowers did not have the capacity to repay and yet pushed loans on to them. For example, the executives at Countrywide, a nonbank lender, recognized that that many of the loans they were originating could have "catastrophic consequences."[33] Leading financial institutions knew that they were not properly sampling the loans that they were purchasing and packaging for sale to others. They were aware that some of the loans they had sampled were not meeting their underwriting standards or those of the originators. Nevertheless, they went ahead with the purchases. In the originate-to-distribute model, there were no strong incentives for originators and those packaging the loans for sale to ensure quality of loans originated.

There were significant failures of risk management. Banks held on their books large amounts of highly correlated housing assets. They held too little capital: the ratio of debt to equity was as high as 35:1. There was excessive dependence on short-term borrowings.[34] The deposit to asset ratio is a measure of the dependence on banks on short-term borrowings; the lower the ratio, the greater is the dependence.

In the United States, the United Kingdom, France, Germany, and several other countries, the ratio fell between 2004 and 2006. The ratio was between 50 and 60 percent in both the United States and the United Kingdom, which points to a high dependence on external funds. At 10 large publicly traded banks in the United States, the ratio came down from around 43 percent to a little over 35 percent.[35]

Top management at many banks did not want to hear warnings from those below. In many banks, those who urged caution and tried to alert senior management to the risks involved ended up paying a price. The head of fixed income at Lehman Brothers, who warned against taking on too much risk, had to leave. At Citigroup, a banker, who found that as much as 60 percent of the loans Citibank was purchasing were defective, saw his bonus reduced and was downgraded in his performance review.[36]

Basel Rules

The Bank of International Settlements, based in Basel, Switzerland, has framed rules for capital required for banks. These are known as the Basel rules and are accepted in 100 countries around the world. The first set of rules was framed in 1998. This is known as Basel I. A sequel happened in 2004. These are known as Basel II.

One of the key features of Basel II was allowing banks to lower their capital based on sophisticated risk management models that enabled them to lower their risk, provided these models had been duly validated by the regulator. However, these models are often based on past data. We know from experience that such models can break down in the face of "black swan" events, that is, events that depart significantly from what has happened in the past. When this happens, it turns out that the capital set aside by a bank is inadequate to cope with the situation.

Second, the rules were drawn up in such a way that the aggregate capital requirements did not increase relative to Basel I. This was done so that the banking system as a whole was not required to raise additional capital. It was felt that if the banking system were compelled to raise more capital and had difficulty in doing so, it would respond by reducing the size of the balance sheet and this would result in a credit crunch. For both these reasons, when the crisis of 2007 happened, there was not enough capital in the banking system to deal with losses.

Third, Basel rules required traded assets to be marked to market. We know that, in times of panic, prices tend to overshoot. As a result, assets that are marked to market can inflict very large losses during the period that panic lasts. This happened during the financial crisis of 2007. It was one reason why equity at banks was eroded badly or wiped out. We will elaborate on this point a little later in this chapter.

Fourth, the Basel II rules were pro-cyclical, that is, they tended to reinforce business fluctuations. During an upturn, banks would lend more and make more profit, which would boost capital through retained earnings. The boost to capital, in turn, would enable banks to lend even more. During a downturn, lower credit growth and losses on loans would tend to erode capital. Lower capital would mean lower loan growth, which would reinforce the downturn, which, in turn, would exacerbate bank losses.

While all of these criticisms of Basel II are theoretically valid, the fact remains that implementation of Basel II in the United States was deferred until 2010 and involved a limited number of banks. In the European Union too, use of Basel II was limited in 2007 when the crisis erupted.

However, two points made about the Basel rules are valid. They allowed banks to get away with too little equity capital even under Basel I. Second, mark-to-market requirements caused banks to suffer huge losses on their trading portfolio. This caused a significant erosion of bank capital and even led to many failures.

Credit Rating Agencies

The U.S. housing boom that started in the late-1990s and continued until 2006 was fuelled substantially by subprime mortgage lending. The finance for these loans came through a process of securitization. Banks packaged subprime loans into mortgage-backed securities. They had senior and junior tranches. The junior tranches were expected to bear the loss first in the event of default. Investors, including banks and other financial institutions, invested large amounts of money in senior tranches.

Banks and financial institutions created structured investment vehicles (SIVs) that invested in these securities backed by issuing commercial paper. Since the securities had high ratings, the commercial paper used to finance investment in these also carried high ratings, which made it cheaper for the SIVs to borrow.

Consider the case of a securitization in 2006 that involved Citibank.[37] The deal involved $947 million in mortgage-backed bonds. New Century Financial sold 4,499 mortgages to Citibank which sold them to a separate legal entity sponsored by Citibank and that would own the mortgages and issue securities against these. The Citibank entity divided the mortgages, which carried the rights to borrowers' monthly payments, into 17 tranches.

The credit rating agencies assigned ratings to most of these tranches. The four senior tranches were rated AAA. Below the senior tranches were 11 "mezzanine" tranches, whose risk was between that of the senior and lowest tranches. Three of these tranches were rated AA, three were A, three were BBB, and two were BB or junk. The junior-most tranche was called the "equity" or "first-loss" tranche as it would suffer the first losses on any default on the mortgages in the pool. Investors in the lowest tranches received the highest interest rates corresponding to the high risk carried by these. The highest tranches were the safest. In this deal, 78 percent of the securities was rated AAA.

There were clear incentives for banks to invest in such securities instead of holding mortgages as loans. If the banks had $100 in mortgage loans, they would have to set aside $5 in capital. If they converted the loans into securities, sold the securities in tranches and then bought all the tranches, they would have to hold about $4.10.

This was not the end of the story. The lowest-rated tranches in securitization deals might be hard to sell despite their higher yields. A market had to be found for them. Wall Street found an answer: Collateralized Debt Obligations (CDOs). These involved taking the BBB or A-grade tranches from various securitization deals and packaging them into a new set of securities. The CDO securities would have the same structure as mortgage-backed securities, with senior, middle, and lower tranches.

About 80 percent of the CDOs so created would again be AAA rated despite the fact that they comprised low grade tranches from other securitization deals. This neat trick was explained by diversification. Since the BBB securities that went into CDOs were drawn from different pools, they would not all go bad at the same time. Again, only those at the bottom of the securitization ladder stood to lose. Between 2003 and 2007, as house prices rose 27 percent in the United States and $4 trillion in mortgage-backed securities was created, Wall Street issued nearly $700 billion in CDOs.[38]

Thus, credit rating agencies had a role to play in the housing boom. The securities that financed the boom were bought by banks and financial institutions only on the strength of the high ratings given to them by rating agencies. Regulations require certain financial institutions to invest only in securities of a certain rating. Moreover, the rating agencies had earned a certain credibility over the years through their ratings of government and corporate bonds and commercial paper. Both issuers of securitized assets and investors in these needed the rating agencies. Securitization could not have grown as large as it did without the participation of the credit rating agencies.

The higher the ratings of the securities, the bigger was the market and the greater the profit to those issuing the securities. Thus, the issuers had an interest in getting high ratings. He who pays the paper calls the tune. In the securitized assets market, unlike in the market for government and corporate debt, the issuers were relatively few in number, so they were better placed to put pressure on rating agencies to give high ratings; they could always move their business to a rating agency that was willing to provide a better rating. Moreover, the securities packages that were being rated were more complex than the typical government or corporate bond. It was not easy for outsiders to judge the risk involved, so errors made by rating agencies were unlikely to get picked up by the market quickly.

From 2005 to 2007, Moody's rated nearly 45,000 mortgage-related securities as AAA. Compare this with the fact that, in early 2010, only six private sector companies in the whole of the United States merited AAA rating.[39] The ratings of securities issued in the period 2005–2007, in particular, turned out to be far too optimistic. The rating agencies were also slow to downgrade these securities as the losses became apparent. By June 2009, 90 percent of the collateralized debt obligation tranches issued between 2005 and 2007 had been downgraded with 80 percent being downgraded below investment grade.[40]

America's FCIC concluded:

> The three credit rating agencies were key enablers of the financial meltdown. The mortgage-related securities at the heart of the crisis could not have been marketed and sold without their seal of approval. …
> Their ratings helped the market soar and their downgrades through 2007 and 2008 wreaked havoc across markets and firms.[41]

In 2013, the U.S. Justice Department brought a case against S&P for fraudulently issuing favorable ratings in order to boost its market. In February, 2015, S&P settled the case with a fine of $1.37 billion.[42]

Greedy Consumers

We have shown how the government in the United States did all it could to encourage broader home ownership. The flip side of the coin was a willingness on the part of consumers to plunge into home ownership with little regard for the risks involved. Some of it may have been due to lack of financial literacy. But there was also, in many cases, a willingness to ignore risks.

Subprime loans had happened long before the 2000s. In the 1980s, there were subprime lenders who were willing to make loans to those whom the banks turned away. They made home equity loans to those with troubled financial histories or who lacked credit histories. They charged a higher interest rate to cover the risk but the rate was still lower than on car loans or credit cards.[43] Subprime originations increased from $70 billion in 1996 to $135 billion in 1998 before falling to $100 billion in 2000. In the late-1990s, the share of subprime originations in mortgages was around 10 percent.[44] In 2006, subprime mortgages accounted for 23.5 percent of all mortgage originations.[45]

The subprime market went through a crisis in the late-1990s. Following the Russian Crisis and the collapse of the hedge fund, Long-Term Capital Management, the demand for subprime assets fell. The borrowing costs of subprime originators rose even while the demand for these assets was falling. Several nonbank prime lenders went bankrupt.

As the Fed cut interest rates in the early 2000s, ARMs became very attractive to borrowers. The share of ARMs in prime borrowers rose from 4 percent in 2001 to 10 percent in 2003 and 21 percent in 2004. Among subprime borrowers, the share of ARMs rose from 60 to 76 percent. Nearly a quarter of all mortgages made in the first quarter of 2005 were interest-only loans that allowed them to defer payment of the principal.[46]

As the demand for housing grew, fuelled by attractive rates and other terms, the prices of homes rose along with its household wealth. The top 10 percent of households by net worth saw the value of their homes going up by $77,000 between 2001 and 2004; the bottom 25 percent saw an increase of more than $12,000. The increase in home values fuelled spending by consumers in several ways. One was to refinance homes at lower interest rates (given that interest rates were falling) and collect the difference in interest rates as cash—this was known as cash-out refinancing. Another was to take home equity loans, that is, to borrow against the increase in value of homes.

In 2001–2003, cash-out refinancing netted households an estimated $427 billion; home equity loans $430 billion. One survey showed that 45 percent of who took home equity loans used their money for expenses such as medical bills, taxes, electronics, vacations or to consolidate debt; another 31 percent for home improvements; and the rest for more real estate, cars, investments, clothes, or jewelry.[47]

The down payment on a mortgage had for long been 20 percent (or a loan-to-value ratio, LTV, of 80 percent). As housing prices rose, it became difficult for large numbers of people to make a down payment of this order. Where the down payment was less than 20 percent, borrowers were required to take out mortgage insurance that could compensate lenders in the event of default. This meant that the borrower had to pay fees for insurance that added to the cost of ownership.

Lenders found an answer that borrowers were only too happy to embrace: lower down payments without insurance. Neither Congress nor regulators ever got down to mandating LTV standards for mortgages. Banks resorted to even higher LTV lending, using what are called "piggyback mortgages." They offered a first mortgage for 80 percent of the home value and a second one for 10 or even 20 percent. Borrowers found that the monthly payments on the two mortgages were lower than the monthly payment on a traditional mortgage plus mortgage insurance. With banks and borrowers both loving this product, the average LTV across home mortgages rose from 79 to 86 percent between 2001 and 2006.[48]

Banks also found ways to get people into mortgages with low documentation: They were willing requirements of information if borrowers were willing to pay a higher interest rate. As a result, between 2000 and 2007, low- and no-doc loans rose from less than 2 percent of outstanding loans to 9 percent.[49]

The percentage of borrowers who defaulted on their mortgages within a few months of taking the loan nearly doubled between the summer of 2006 and late-2007. This suggests many took out loans that they did not have the capacity or intention to repay. Overall mortgage indebtedness in the United States rose from $5.3 trillion in 2001 to $10.5 trillion in 2007. The amount of mortgage debt per household rose from $91,500 in 2001 to $149,500 in 2007.[50]

Consumers thus contributed to the subprime crisis through greed or ignorance. They borrowed to finance the purchase of homes in ways that were not prudent.

Regulatory Failure

The financial crisis of 2007 highlighted serious failures of regulation.

Financial firms made home loans based on their appraisal of the value of a home. This put pressure on appraisers to inflate the values of homes they appraised. If a home is selling for $100,000 and an appraiser says it is worth $80,000, then the loan of $90,000 needed to finance the purchase will not come through. Borrowers, lenders, mortgage brokers, lenders all put pressure on appraisers to inflate the value of homes. In 2003, a survey found that 55 percent of the appraisers felt obliged to inflate the value of homes; by 2006, this figure had climbed to 90 percent.

Regulators should have responded to evidence of inflation in the values of homes. They failed to do so. In 1994, The Fed, the FDIC, the Office of Controller of Currency (OCC), and the OTS raised the value of homes that required appraisal by the lenders they regulated from $100,000 to $250,000. There was also a lack of oversight of appraisers. In several states, there was a large increase in the number of appraisers inspite of the lack of qualified trainers.[51]

There were other ways in which lax regulation or relaxations of existing regulations sowed the seeds for the crisis of 2007. The 1982 St Germain Act significantly broadened the types of loans and investments that thrifts could make. Earlier, the thrifts relied on 30-year mortgages. As inflation rose, thrifts were badly impacted by the fixed interest rate to which they were committed. The St Germain Act allowed them to offer new types of loans—interest-rate only, balloon-payment, and ARMs.[52]

An interest-only mortgage allows the borrower to pay only the interest for the set term with the principal amount remaining unchanged during the period; once the term ends, the borrower pay the principal plus interest over the rest of the term. A balloon payment mortgage does not amortize fully over the tenure of the loan, leaving a large residual amount to be paid at the time of maturity. Both these loans reduced the burden of repayment in the short-term but led to higher burdens later. They were convenient to borrowers who expected their income to rise over the years. In an ARM, the interest rate varies over the tenure of the loan depending on the lender's cost of borrowing. Essentially, it allows the lender to pass the interest rate risk on loans to the borrower.

Beginning in 1987, the U.S. Fed began to dilute the provisions of the Glass-Steagall Act of 1933, which prohibited banks from being involved in investment banking activities. Banks were not allowed to underwrite or invest in securities. The scope of "bank-ineligible" activities was gradually expanded until, by 1997, such securities could go up to 25 percent of a bank's assets or revenues. At the same time, the OCC, which regulated banks with a national charter, liberalized norms for banks to participate in derivatives. These measures again flowed from the perception that markets were superior to regulation and that it was best to leave it to market forces to impose the necessary discipline on banks.[53]

In 1999, Congress passed the Gramm-Leach-Bliley Act which lifted most of the remaining provisions of the Glass-Steagall Act. Bank holding companies were now free to sell banking, insurance, and securities products, subject to their meeting requirements of safety and soundness. The 25-percent ceiling on securities affiliates, mentioned previously, was removed.

The argument for Glass-Steagall had been that banks' core functions—taking deposits, making loans, and facilitating payments—should not be endangered by investment banking activities. Various arguments were put forward for the removal of the Glass-Steagall restrictions. Banks would enjoy the benefits of scale and scope, they could lower risk through diversification and they could provide consumers a single-window for all their requirements of financial services.

One consequence of the dismantling of Glass-Steagall was that it weakened regulation of financial holding companies whose activities spanned banking, securities, and insurance. The Fed decided that it would supervise financial holding companies as a whole, looking only at risks that cut across the holding companies—this came to be known as "Fed-Lite." The detailed supervision of each subsidiary would be left to the concerned regulator. Fed Chairman Ben Bernanke was to remark later that Fed-Lite "made it difficult for any single regulator to reliably see the whole picture of activities and risks of large, complex banking institutions."

In the United States, regulation of banks is shared by several authorities. The Fed, the state regulators, and the FDIC supervise the state banks. The OCC supervises national banks. The OTS supervises the thrifts. The Fed had the authority to write clear rules to regulate all types of lenders. In 1969, the Fed adopted regulation Z for the purpose of implementing the Truth in Lending Act of 1968 but enforcement was left to multiple regulators.[54]

What about nonbank subprime lenders? The Fed had the authority to supervise the subprime lending subsidiaries of banks. For other nonbank lenders, authority vested with the Federal Trade Commission (FTC). The FTC, it was seen later, did not have the budget and the staff to adequately do this job.

In 1994, Congress passed the Home Ownership and Equity Protection Act (HOEPA) to address concerns about predatory mortgage lending practices. This was in response to widespread complaints that certain communities were being sold high-rate, high-fee mortgage loans. The legislation banned certain practices such as prepayment penalties, balloon payments on loans with a term of less than 5 years, and basing high-cost refinance loans on the collateral value of the home alone, without taking into account the consumer's repayment capacity.

However, initially, only a small percentage of mortgage loans were covered by the Act because the interest rate and fee levels that triggered its provisions were too high for most subprime loans. In the years that followed, the Fed did not react suitably to evidence of abuses in the mortgage lending market. The abuses included high fees and prepayment penalties, high pressure sales tactics, and a tendency to prey on the elderly, minorities, and those with low incomes. Following evidence of predatory lending practices, the Fed amended introduced rules intended to limit high interest lending and prevent multiple refinancings over a short period of time. It turned out, however, that those rules covered only 1 percent of subprime loans.[55]

It was evident that banks were facing competitive pressures from non-bank lenders in the subprime market. The answer was to put in place clear rules that ensured that, in such cases, the consumer had the capacity to repay when the interest rate got reset. However, neither Congress nor the Fed was willing to take the necessary action for fear that any measures to correct abuses would come in the way of home ownership for the poor.

When Citigroup acquired Associates First, the second biggest subprime lender, the move was opposed by consumer groups who saw Associates First as a predatory lender. However, regulators approved the acquisition. The Fed resisted attempts on the part of its staff to examine practices at the nonbank subsidiaries of Citigroup.[56] Again, the problem was the philosophy that regulation should be light and that it should be left to the market to correct excesses.

Mortgage lenders took to financing themselves through commercial paper, Asset Backed Commercial Paper (ABCP). The share of ABCP in all commercial paper rose from 25 to 50 percent between 1997 and 2001. Commercial banks found they could reduce their capital requirements by parking mortgages in off-balance sheet entities backed by commercial paper. Mortgages on the balance sheet required banks to set aside 4 percent in capital. However, in off-balance sheet entities, there was no charge. In 2004, the regulators introduced a modest charge of 0.8 percent toward capital for off-balance sheet entities.[57]

The FCIC concluded, "Regulators failed to rein risky home mortgage lending. In particular, the Federal Reserve failed to meet its statutory obligation to establish and maintain prudent mortgage lending standards and to protect against predatory lending."[58]

Why did regulators not frame and enforce strict regulations that would have prevented the race to the bottom? Well, they understood full well that the goal of spreading home ownership had broad political support in Washington. They could see that the growth of home ownership was creating jobs and incomes. They did not want to antagonize the powerful financial sector lobby. And they did not think that the financial system would crumble if the housing sector ran into trouble.

We have mentioned the role of derivatives, such as securitized products, in causing the crisis. Regulation contributed in this area as well. In December 2000, Congress passed the Commodity Futures Modernization Act (CFMA) which substantially deregulated the OTC derivatives market and eliminated oversight by the Commodities Futures Trading Commission (CFTC) and the Securities and Exchange Commission (SEC).[59]

Which Factor Was Primarily Responsible for the Crisis?

This completes our portrait gallery of the principal villains in the crisis. Such a depiction is convenient because it allows those in authority to disclaim responsibility. If blame can be spread across several villains, no one villain need be brought to book. Such an approach is not useful, however, in preventing "crime" in the future. Since many of these factors are bound to recur, we must reconcile ourselves to such crises happening in the future as well.

The difficulty with the Murder-on-the Orient-Express theory is that some of the factors we have listed have existed in the past and in other places without bringing on a major global crisis. For instance, there have been periods of low and falling interest rates earlier. Several countries have had housing bubbles. But these did not translate into a financial crisis in the countries concerned.

Political pressure to widen home ownership was certainly a factor. Politicians will always want institutions to pursue goals that they think will fetch votes. But it does not follow that banks or GSEs have to oblige them. Politicians often want companies to create jobs in particular areas, they are averse to companies moving jobs overseas and they oppose closures or layoffs that will result in job losses. Companies do not make it a point to oblige politicians in these matters.

Some have blamed "shadow banking," the existence of unregulated or lightly regulated players in the financial sector, for the crisis. We do know, however, that failure was not confined to investment banks such as Bear Stearns or Lehman Brothers or mortgage originators such as Countrywide. Banks, such as Citigroup, that straddled commercial banking and investment banking failed. So did pure commercial banks, such as Northern Rock in the United States as also an insurance company, American International Group (AIG).

Similarly, greedy bankers and consumers cannot be the explanation for the simple reason that greed is not new to mankind. The two GSEs, we have seen, contributed to the crisis but, as we have argued, cannot be said to be the primary cause. Securitization was not invented in the years preceding the crisis, so it's hard to hold it primarily responsible for the crisis.

We need a more nuanced understanding of the financial crisis, one that focuses on the primary or most important cause. In what follows, I will attempt to provide one.

Let us focus on subprime loans, from which the crisis is widely believed to have originated. As Table 2.3 shows, the losses from housing loans *per se* were not very large. In October 2008, the IMF estimated loan losses of financial institutions at $425 billion. Of these, bank losses were estimated at $255–290 billion. Subprime loan losses were only $50 billion and alt-A loan losses $35 billion or a total of $85 billion. One could ascribe a small portion of losses on other categories of loans, such as prime loans, commercial real estate and consumer loans, to the adverse

Table 2.3 Financial institutions' losses on loans

$ billion			
	Loans	**Losses**	**% loss**
Subprime	300	50	17%
Alt-A	600	35	6%
Prime	3,800	85	2%
Comml real estate	2,400	90	4%
Consumer	1,400		
All loans	12,370	**425**	3%
Total bank losses $255–290			
Financial institutions' losses on securities			
	Loans	**Losses**	**% loss**
Asset Backed Securities (ABS)	1,100	210	19%
ABS CDOs	400	290	73%
Total securities	10,840	980	9%
Loans and securities	23,210	1405	6%
Bank losses on securities: $725–820 bn			

Source: IMF, Global Financial Stability Report, October 2008, p. 12.

conditions created by the defaults on subprime loans. Yet, total loan losses were not large enough to drag down the banks or the financial system.

It was the losses on securities held by financial institutions that really made the difference. Total losses on securities held by financial institutions were $980 billion (with bank losses amounting to $725–820 billion). Losses on asset-backed securities and asset-backed CDOs (most of which may be presumed to be mortgage-backed and with a subprime component) amounted to $500 billion. In addition, some of the losses on other securities may be ascribed to the market conditions arising from losses on subprime-related securities.

Thus, the losses on subprime and alt-A loans could have been absorbed by banks and financial institutions. It was the losses on subprime related securities that proved devastating. It was financial institutions investing their liabilities in securities that contained subprime loans, not so much in the subprime loans themselves, that was primarily responsible for the magnitude of the losses and the crisis that followed. As the then

Chairman of the Fed, Ben Bernanke, put it at that time, "Subprime mortgages themselves are a pretty small asset class.... But what created the contagion, or one of the things that created the contagion, was that the subprime mortgages were entangled in these huge securitized pools."[60]

There is a reason why holding loans in the form of securitized products proved lethal. Securities are marked to market, so the full magnitude of losses is realized instantaneously. In contrast, loans are subject to provisions with the full magnitude of losses showing up over a longer period. Mark-to-market accounting was thus crucial to the size of the losses inflicted on financial institutions.

Further, banks had funded their investment in securities very substantially in the wholesale market. When wholesale funding dried up in the panic that ensued, banks had to liquidate some of the securities they held. This caused prices to fall further and increased mark-to-market losses. There was no market for some of the securities, hence no market prices were available. Losses had to be estimated by methods that tend to exaggerate the losses, meaning the prices thrown up by those methods were lower than those warranted by the default rates on the loans embedded in the securities.

We can discern two issues in the analysis presented earlier. One was the extent of securitization which allowed originators of loans to palm off low-quality loans to others through packages of securities that received high ratings from the rating agencies. The other is the propensity of financial institutions to hold securities rather than loans on their books. Following the example of investment banks that reported high returns on equity by focusing on trading income, banks had chosen to increase the proportion of securities on their books in relation to conventional loans. In other words, banks had chosen to behave more like investment banks rather than commercial banks.

Thus, the serious failures in relation to banks were: lowering of loan writing standards; a focus on trading income by holding securitized assets; accepting securitized assets that contained low-quality loans thanks to the high ratings these received from rating agencies; dependence on wholesale funds to finance investments; and low amounts of equity capital in relation assets. Every one of these involves regulatory failure. Thus, in our view, *the subprime crisis was primarily a failure of regulation.*

A Different View: The House of Debt

There is a view that the subprime crisis reflected flaws in the financial system that went beyond the failure of regulation as it is commonly understood. On this view, the problem was not fundamentally the failure of banks at all. The problem was the explosion of private debt in the system. This is a radically different perspective on the financial crisis.

In their book, *The House of Debt*, Atif Mian and Amir Sufi argue that subprime crisis was primarily the result of a sharp increase in private debt—that is, the debt of households and of nonfinancial firms—in the years preceding the crisis. This increase was fuelled by an expansion of credit from financial firms.[61]

Debt was used by households to invest in houses. When housing prices collapsed, the net worth of borrowers fell sharply. The fall in net worth, in turn, led to a steep cut in consumption. The recession, the authors argue, followed from a collapse in demand and not from the failure of banks. This thesis needs elaboration.

Let us begin with the explosion of debt. The authors note that the U.S. household debt doubled in the period 2000–2007 to $14 trillion and the debt to household income ratio rose sharply from 1.4 to 2.1 Something similar had happened before the Great Depression of the last century—outstanding mortgages for nonfarm properties tripled from 1920 to 1929. They point to another common element in the two recessions: both were preceded by a drop in household spending.[62]

A similar pattern is observed in the 16 OECD economies. They cite a study that showed that countries with the largest increase in debt from 1997 to 2007 were the ones that suffered the largest decline in spending from 2008 to 2009. The increase in household debt in six countries (Ireland, Denmark, the United Kingdom, Spain, Portugal, and the Netherlands) was even greater than in the United States. And in five of these countries, the drop in household spending was even greater.

Another study (by the IMF) extended the analysis to 36 countries, including many East European and Asian countries. This study also showed that the rise in household debt is one of the best predictors of the decline in household spending during the recession.

How does the buildup of household debt impact consumption? Mian and Sufi point out that households have two forms of assets: financial and housing assets. Net worth is the total of financial assets and housing assets minus debt. Mortgages and home equity debt (borrowing against one's share in the value of a house) constitute the biggest chunk of household debt in the United States—80 percent in 2006.[63]

Households in the United States differ both in respect of the amount of net worth they have and the amount of debt or leverage. For the poorest households—those at the bottom 20 percent in the distribution of net worth—leverage measured as the ratio of debt to total assets was 80 percent. Moreover, $4 out of $5 of their net worth was in home equity—in other words, they had little by way of financial assets.

In contrast, rich households—those at the top 20 percent of the distribution of net worth—had a leverage ratio of only 7 percent. They had only $1 out of every $5 in home equity, meaning they were heavily invested in financial assets.

We have seen earlier that there was a steep fall in housing prices from 2006 to 2009. Since the poor's net worth was mostly in home equity, they were hit very hard. The effect was magnified by their high leverage. The authors illustrate this point with the help of a simple example.

Assume an individual finances a $100,000 house with $20,000 of his own equity and a mortgage of $80,000. He then has a leverage of 80 percent. If home prices drop by 20 percent, his net worth, which was $20,000 to start with, gets wiped out. In other words, a 20-percent drop in home prices translates into 100-percent drop in net worth. This is the effect of leverage. Thus, poor households with net worth almost entirely in home equity and with high leverage stand to lose the most when home prices fall.

This is precisely what happened when home prices fell by 30 percent from 2006 to 2009. The net worth of the poorest 20 percent fell from $30,000 to 0 in the period 2006–2010. In contrast, the net worth of rich households fell from $3.6 million to $2.9 million.

The erosion in net worth of the poorer households resulted in a decline in consumption. This decline in consumption, the authors argue, preceded the peak of the banking crisis, which was marked by the collapse of Lehman Brothers in September 2008. They cite the following facts in respect of consumption:[64]

- Retail items such as auto spending, furniture spending, and home improvement spending showed sharp declines in the period January to August 2008 relative to the same period in 2007.
- In the third and fourth quarters of 2008, overall consumption declined by 5.2 percent. Combining this with the previous fact, they conclude that "the collapse in consumption began before the end of 2008, but it no doubt accelerated during the banking crisis."
- In the third quarter of 2008, the collapse of GDP was the result of a fall in consumption. The effect of nonresidential investment, that is, investment by businesses was less than half that of consumption.
- It was not until the first and second quarters of 2009 that the contribution of business investment to growth was most negative.

The authors conclude that household spending was the "key driver of the recession, not the effects of the banking crisis on businesses." The banking crisis merely amplified the effects of household consumption.

Analysis of data at the microlevel substantiates their view. If their hypothesis—that the erosion in net worth due to high levels of indebtedness was the principal cause of the recession—is right, household spending should have fallen more steeply in areas where housing net worth fell the most. This is precisely what happened. The authors also found that the highest fall in net worth happened in places that had a combination of a high fall in housing prices and high debt levels.

The rise in debt was caused by a huge expansion in credit in the years preceding the crisis. For 2002–2005, Mian and Sufi found that credit expansion in low credit score zip codes was 30 percent whereas it was only 11 percent for high credit score zip codes. In other words, marginal borrowers found it easier now to get credit than in the past.[65]

What caused lenders to push credit into those with low scores? Was it because economic fundamentals had improved and this had caused a boom in housing prices? Or was it the expansion in credit that caused the housing bubble in the first place? If fundamentals had improved, credit expansion should have happened in response to an increase in income of marginal borrowers. However, data showed that throughout America, credit was flowing in larger amounts into low credit-score zip codes where income growth was declining. In 2002–2005, mortgage credit growth and income growth were negatively correlated.[66]

We mentioned earlier Robert Shiller's view that an irrational housing bubble came into being and that, in expanding credit, lenders were responding to higher housing prices. The authors examine the question: Was it the housing bubble that caused an expansion in credit or was it the other way around?

The authors attempt to answer the question by comparing credit expansion in cities with elastic supply of housing with that in cities with inelastic supply of housing. In places, where the supply of housing is elastic, that is the supply of housing responds to higher demand, there should be no housing bubble. This is duly confirmed by data. In 2001–2006, housing prices rose by almost 100 percent in inelastic cities where they rose by only 40 percent in elastic cities.[67]

If a housing bubble were driving credit expansion, there should be a large expansion in credit only in inelastic cities and not in elastic cities. It turns out that significant credit expansion in low credit-score zip codes also happened in cities with elastic supply of housing. In inelastic cities, the credit expansion caused a housing bubble; in elastic cities, it did not. These facts, the authors argue, clearly indicate that it was credit expansion that fuelled the housing boom and not *vice versa*.

There was one other factor that exacerbated the crisis. As home prices rose, home owners borrowed against the higher prices and use the money for consumption. In inelastic cities, where home prices rose more, home owners increased their debt by 55 percent compared to the increase of 25 percent inelastic cities. The authors write, "The incredibly aggressive borrowing by home owners was instrumental in causing the U.S. household-debt crisis." Without their borrowing, the economy would not have suffered as much as it did.[68]

In sum, it was the increase in household debt made possible by credit expansion that was primarily responsible for the magnitude of the Great Recession. The failure of banks may have exacerbated the crisis but it was not the primary cause.

Does this refute our thesis that regulation of banks was the principal failure that led to the crisis? No, it doesn't. It only shows that the ambit of regulation has to be much broader than it has been. Bank regulation must limit the expansion of credit and it must also ensure that credit flow into particular sectors, such as real estate, should not be excessive. We address this and other issues related to bank regulation in Chapter 5.

Summary

We have examined the Murder-on-the-Orient-Express theory of the financial crisis. According to this theory, at least a dozen reasons can be found for the crisis. These are: a housing bubble in the United States and elsewhere; political pressure in the United States to expand the supply of home loans; global macroeconomic imbalances; loose monetary policies; excessive financialization; belief in market efficiency; Fannie Mae and Freddie Mac, two government-sponsored entities; greedy and incompetent bankers and financiers; Basel rules; credit rating agencies; greedy consumers; regulatory failure.

This is not terribly helpful because if so many factors were responsible, there is, perhaps, little that policy can do about it. Our own view is that the crisis was primarily a failure of regulation. Poor regulation made possible lax underwriting standards. It allowed banks to operate with too little capital and with an excess of short-term borrowings. It permitted banks to focus excessively on trading assets that were subject to mark-to-market accounting. It did little to impose discipline on rating agencies that rated securitized assets.

However, it would be incorrect to view the financial crisis as arising from a failure of banks alone. The underlying cause was an excessive buildup of private debt. This led to a housing bubble and the bursting of the bubble rendered banks vulnerable and worsened the crisis. This, however, does not detract from our view that regulatory failure was the principal failure in the crisis. It only means that the ambit of regulation must be widened to prevent excessive buildup of private debt. We elaborate on this idea in Chapter 5.

CHAPTER 3

Regulatory Reform Since the Crisis

We saw in Chapter 2 that the Great Recession of 2007–09 in the United States, which continues to impact the rest of the world, was at least in part the result of multiple bank failures and bank crises in the leading economies of the world. Much of the regulatory reform has, accordingly, focused on finding ways to strengthen banks so that they are less vulnerable to a crisis.

In what follows, we look at some of the important regulatory responses to the crisis. These are, for the most part, relatively straightforward and controversial. They address aspects of the crisis that are fairly amenable to resolution. The more difficult part of bank regulation, which is the too-big-to-fail problem, and the more unorthodox solutions to financial crises we shall consider in Chapters 4 and 5 respectively.

Some of the important regulatory responses to issues in banking are:

    i. Higher capital requirements for banks
    ii. Higher liquidity requirements
   iii. Improved bank governance
    iv. Changes in remuneration policy for bank executives
    v. Macroprudential regulation
    vi. Evaluating the role of rating agencies
   vii. Norms for securitization
  viii. Addressing global imbalances and global regulation

In what follows, we take up each of these responses in turn.

Higher Capital Requirements for Banks

Basel III Norms

Banks suffered huge losses in the crisis of 2007. Many did not have adequate capital to weather the losses. As a result, they failed. The first and most obvious response, therefore, has to be to address the amount of capital that banks are required to hold. This is precisely what regulators have attempted to do. The result is a new set of rules for bank capital that is called Basel III.[1] These rules are expected to come into force in their entirety by 2019.

Basel III has several objectives:

- Increase the amount of risk capital banks hold
- Improve the quality of capital that banks hold
- Broaden the risks that banks are expected to cover
- Supplement risk-based capital with an accounting ratio to capture the proportion of capital on the balance sheet
- Reduce cyclicality in bank lending
- Address systemic risk

Before we get into the details of Basel III, a word about the Basel norms would be in order. Under the Basel norms, banks are required to hold capital against various assets in their portfolio. However, capital is held, not against the nominal value of the asset, but what is called the "risk-weighted" value. This is based on the fact that not all assets carry equal risk. Government bonds were believed to be largely risk-free and hence carried a risk weight of 0 percent. At the other end, a corporate loan carries a risk weight of 100 percent because the entire value can be lost if the borrower defaults. In between, we have items such as mortgages that carry a risk weight of 50 percent.

Banks are required to multiply each asset by the weight assigned to it by the regulator and compute the total risk-weighted assets. Against this total, banks must hold capital. The capital is of two forms, Tier 1 and Tier 2. Tier 1 consists of common equity and securities, such as perpetual preferred stock, that have many features of common equity. Tier 2 capital consists of subordinated debt, perpetual debt, hybrid capital instruments, and so on. Under Basel II, banks were required to hold total capital (Tier 1 plus Tier 2) to the extent of 8 percent of total risk-weighted assets. Tier 1 capital was required to be at least 4 percent of the total and the balance could be Tier 2 capital.

Under Basel III, several changes to capital requirements have been made:

- Tier 1 capital will have to be 6 percent out of the earlier total capital of 8 percent. Of the 6 percent capital in Tier 1, 4.5 percent has to be common equity. Thus, the quality of capital required improves considerably under Basel III.
- Banks will also have to provide a "capital conservation buffer" in the form of common equity of 2.5 percent. Banks can distribute dividends freely only if they have the capital conservation buffer in full. To the extent that there is shortfall in the buffer, that is, common equity is in the range 4.5 to less than 7 percent, they can distribute dividends only in accordance with a restrictive schedule prescribed by the regulators.
- Banks will also be required to have a "countercyclical buffer" in the form of common equity of 0–2.5 percent of risk-weighted assets as prescribed by the regulator. As the name suggests, these are intended to slow down growth in assets when the economy is booming and support growth in assets when the economy is in a downturn.
- "Systemically important banks," that is, banks whose failure can disrupt the entire system will be required to hold an additional 2.5 percent of capital as common equity.
- Lastly, regulators will be free to prescribe a leverage ratio, that is, a ratio of equity to total assets in addition to the norms for risk-weighted capital. At a minimum, this will be 3 percent. However, the Bank for International Settlements (BIS) has indicated that this could rise. The United States insists on a ratio of 5 percent for the biggest bank holding companies.

Table 3.1 captures these requirements, except for the capital requirement for systemically important banks.

Table 3.1 *Basel III capital requirements*

Capital requirements and buffers (all numbers in percent)			
	Common equity Tier 1	Tier 1 capital	Total capital
Minimum	4.5	6.0	8.0
Conservation buffer	2.5		
Minimum plus conservation buffer	7.0	8.5	10.5
Countercyclical buffer range	0–2.5		

How does all this change the total capital requirement for banks? Well, we can see that the capital requirement for banks could rise from the present 8 to 13 percent (minimum of 8 percent plus 2.5 percent as capital conservation buffer plus 2.5 percent as countercyclical buffer). Systemically important banks could require another 2.5 percent, which means the total for them could rise to 15.5 percent.

Is Capital Required Under Basel III Norms Adequate?

Do Basel III norms ensure that banks will have enough capital to weather a crisis of the sort we saw in 2007? Following the crisis, the United States estimated that 19 banks needed to hold 8.1 percent of Tier 1 capital to avoid breaching the minimum capital requirement of 4 percent, that is, they needed about 4 percentage points more than the minimum Tier 1 capital.[2]

If we factor in a minimum Tier 1 capital requirement of 6 percent, it means banks would require 10.1 percent of Tier 1 capital. Under Basel III, including the capital conservation and countercyclical buffers, banks would have 11 percent of Tier 1 capital-enough, it seems, to cope with a crisis such as the one in 2007.

This is a rather simplistic view to take. Given that the sample covered only 19 banks, this means that a few banks in the United States would have withstood the crisis of 2007 had they had the higher capital required under Basel III. It does not mean that banks, in general, will be safe under Basel III. This is because leverage ratio under Basel III can be as low as 3 percent, which means that banks can still operate at a debt to equity ratio of 33:1. At such a level of leverage, it requires only a 3 percent drop in the value of assets for a bank to fail.

What, then, would be a safe level of leverage for banks? Common sense suggests that it has to be much lower than 33:1. What would be the case for allowing banks to operate at a level of leverage as high as this and not bringing leverage down to safer levels?

In their book, *The Bankers' New Clothes*, Anat Admati and Martin Hellwig make short work of the arguments made for allowing banks to operate at the present levels of leverage, levels that would be thought preposterous in any other industry.[3] One argument made for high leverage in banking is that debt is cheaper than equity. So, if banks are allowed to have higher levels of debt, it lowers their cost of capital. To the extent that banks' cost of capital is kept low, loans become cheaper. Society benefits as a result: the lower the interest rate, the greater is the investment.

Students of corporate finance should be able to tell that this line of argument is flawed. The cost of debt is not independent of the level of debt. As debt rises, so does its cost. The cost of equity is not independent of the level of debt either. As debt rises, equity holders perceive that their risks have gone up. They demand a higher return than before.

This is the basis for the Modigliani-Miller proposition which states that, under the assumption of perfect capital markets, the cost of capital is independent of the capital structure. Having higher debt should not make any difference to the cost of capital. However, given market imperfections such as taxes, it is true that debt is advantaged over equity. This is because interest costs are tax deductible whereas equity costs are not. But this does not mean that a firm can carry as much as debt as it likes. Beyond a certain level, the cost of bankruptcy overwhelms the tax shield provided by debt.

Now, for a nonfinancial firm, the bankruptcy costs become significant debt to equity ratios of 2:1 or 3:1. It does not make sense for them to borrow beyond this level or the market may simply not be willing to lend to them beyond this level. In the case of banks, the markets tolerate a higher level of debt because of implicit government guarantees for bank debt. Banks enjoy deposit insurance. This means that depositors are protected (up to a specified level of deposits) when banks fail. Knowing that they are protected, depositors (who are lenders to banks) are willing to put up with a higher level of leverage.

Yet another subsidy for banks arises from the "too-big-to-fail" syndrome and this subsidy extends beyond depositors to holders of bonds. We noted in Chapter 1 that governments are unwilling to let large banks fail because of the huge costs that such failures impose on the economy.

Lenders, including those who subscribe to bonds issued by banks, know this and are again willing to tolerate absurdly high levels of leverage. They are not averse to banks operating at absurdly high levels of leverage because, in the event of failure, they expect the banks to be bailed out by the government. So, here's the answer to the puzzle of why banks can afford to operate at high levels of debt: *Debt issued by banks operating at high levels of leverage turns out to be cheap for banks because the costs of high debt are transferred to society at large.*

A second argument made for higher levels of debt—one that we noted in Chapter 2—is that it translates into higher return on equity. This is one reason banks chose to maintain high levels of leverage before the crisis. Bankers' rewards were tied to high return on equity and it suited them to keep leverage as high as possible.

Students of corporate finance should be able to spot the fallacy in this line of thinking. When the level of debt goes up for a given amount of equity, the return on equity goes up, no doubt. But the return on equity *expected* by investors also goes up because equity has become riskier now. Similarly, when debt falls, the return on equity goes down but investors also expect a lower return on equity, given that equity is less risky now.

This makes nonsense of bankers' contention that requiring them to hold more equity and reduce debt will make it harder for them to meet the target for return on equity that investors set for banks. This target, it should be clear, is not set in stone. It depends on how much debt banks are carrying. Carrying a lower level of debt will reduce the return on equity *expected* by investors even as it lowers the *actual* return on equity.

Admati and Hellwig do not set much store by the increase in capital for risk-weighted assets proposed by Basel III norms. They believe that capital, measured simply as the ratio of capital to assets, needs to go up drastically. They believe that banks will be safe only when equity is

20–30 percent of assets. This would mean a debt-to-equity ratio in the range of 3.3–5:1. Compare this with the Basel prescription of a debt-to-equity ratio of 33:1 and you get a good idea of how far banks need to travel to meet the Admati-Hellwig prescription.

The authors contend that the increase in equity capital they recommend involves no cost to society at all. This may not be entirely true. Having banks increase their equity capital does impose costs. It does mean an increase in the cost of capital of banks which translates into higher lending rates.

The BIS has estimated the cost of the higher capital requirements imposed by Basel III norms.[4] If higher capital requirements are phased in over four years, the BIS estimates that each one percentage point increase in bank's actual ratio of tangible common equity to risk-weighted assets will lead to a decline in the level of GDP relative to its baseline path by about 0.09 percent in the steady state.

The benefit is the reduction in the expected cost of a crisis thanks to higher capital requirements. The reduction in the expected cost, in turn, is the product of the probability of a crisis and cost of a crisis. The BIS estimates, for instance, that a 1-percent reduction in the probability of a crisis reduces the annual median cost of a banking crisis by 0.2 percent of output if the effect is temporary. If the effect is long-lasting, the reduction in the annual median cost of a crisis is in the range of 0.6–1.6 percent of output. Next, the BIS estimates the impact of an increase in capital on the probability of a crisis—how much the probability goes down with each percentage increase in the level of capital.

Finally, the BIS computes the net benefit of higher capital requirement—the difference between the reduced loss of output on account of a lower probability of a crisis and the reduced growth rate because of higher capital—as the level of capital is increased. This is captured in Figure 3.1 below. The horizontal axis shows the increase in the capital ratio. The vertical axis gives the net benefit as measured by the percentage impact on the level of output. The red line gives the net benefit when a crisis has moderate permanent effects. The green line gives the net benefit when a crisis has temporary effects.

Figure 3.1 shows that the net benefit of higher capital requirement is positive for increases in risk-weighted capital, starting from a level of

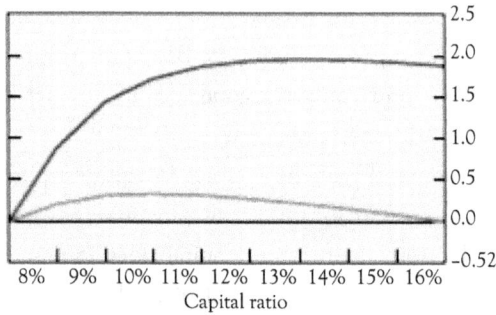

Figure 3.1 BIS estimate of net benefit of increased risk-weighted capital

7 percent and going up to 15 percent. The incremental benefits become negative beyond a certain level of capital.

This estimate hinges crucially on the extent to which each percentage point increase in risk-weighted capital would reduce the probability of a crisis. The BIS estimates imply that the higher risk-weighted capital requirements contemplated under Basel III reduce the probability of a crisis significantly.

Admati and Hellwig would probably disagree. They would point out that the leverage ratio under Basel III rises only from 2 to 3 percent. Their own estimate for a comfortable leverage ratio—that is, a leverage ratio that would make the banking system safer—is 20 to 30 percent. An increase in the ratio of capital to risk-weighted assets even up to 15 percent would not translate into a reduction in leverage of the order intended by Admati and Hellwig. Hence, in their view, it would not mean a significant reduction in the probability of a crisis.

Higher Liquidity Requirements for Banks

We saw in Chapter 2 that one important reason that banks and other financial institutions failed in the financial crisis of 2007 was excessive dependence on short-term funds. A classic case was the failure of the bank Northern Rock in the United Kingdom.

This failure showed that a bank's failure need not arise from the quality of assets alone. It can fail because it does not have sufficiently stable sources of funding and liquid assets that enable it to cope with any shocks to its funding.

Basel III has provisions to address this problem.[5] It requires banks to have adequate liquidity over a 30-day horizon and over a period of more than 1 year as well.

Liquidity over a 30-day horizon is sought to be ensured through the Liquidity Coverage Ratio (LCR).

$$\text{LCR} = \frac{\text{Stock of high quality liquid assets}}{\text{Total net cash flows over the next 30 days}}$$

Basel III stipulates that LCR ≥ 100%

A crucial issue is what constitutes "high quality liquid assets" in the numerator. Basel III identifies three broad groups that qualify:

- Level 1 assets: These include cash, central bank reserves, and top-rated sovereign debt.
- Level 2A assets: These include lower-rated public bonds and higher-rated corporate bonds. These assets must not exceed 40 percent of the total liquid assets and have to been given a "haircut" of 15 percent, that is, they should be valued at 85 percent of the nominal value.
- Level 2B assets: These include lower-rated nonfinancial corporate debt, highly rated equities (each inviting a haircut of 50 percent) and high quality residential MBS (with a haircut of 25 percent). Level 2B assets should not constitute more than 15 percent of the total.

While this classification seems sensible, one cannot always be sure of what constitutes "high quality" assets, especially Level 1 assets that require no haircut. We know how quickly sovereign debt as well as corporate debt can be downgraded. However high the quality of an asset, it would not prudent for banks to take excessive exposure to these. Liquidity is best ensured when banks have a diversified portfolio of high quality liquid assets.

There's another problem with getting banks to hold highly liquid assets. If banks are forced to hold large amounts liquid assets such as government bonds, then it could have the perverse effect of reducing liquidity for want of active trading in these assets. It would be worthwhile, therefore, not to have too narrow a definition of liquidity. Liquid assets may be identified using market indicators such as the bid-ask spread, average issue size, turnover, volatility, and so on.[6]

In addressing LCR, it is important for banks to focus on both the numerator and the denominator. They must ensure that they have sufficiently liquid assets. They must also ensure that there is stability on the funding side, that is, they are not too dependent on wholesale or financial market funding. Financial markets can "freeze up" without warning, that is, supply of funds can dry up. Retail deposits tend to be more stable. The greater the proportion of retail deposits in liabilities, the less vulnerable a bank is to liquidity shocks.

Liquidity over a one year horizon is sought to be ensured through the Net Stable Funding (NSF) ratio.

$$NSF = \frac{\text{Available amount of funding}}{\text{Required amount of funding}}$$

Basel III stipulates that NSF ≥ 100%

Stable funding consists of equity capital, preferred stock and other liabilities of greater than maturity of one year, and so on. Required funding is the sum of value of the assets held multiplied by a required stable funding (RSF) factor. The RSF factor is determined based on amount of a particular asset that could not be monetized through sale or use of collateral on an extended basis during a liquidity event lasting more than one year. BIS has specified RSF factors for various assets, for example, zero for cash zero, 5 percent for marketable securities that are claims on sovereigns, and so on.

Improved Bank Governance

In the years preceding the crisis, bankers had every incentive to take undue risks in pursuit of higher returns. We talked about this in the previous chapter. Several questions have been asked. What were the boards doing? Why did the boards not restrain top management? Did the boards have an adequate appreciation of the levels of risk that their banks were taking?

Governance in banking has thus emerged as an area in which reform is required. Several areas of weaknesses in the boards of banks have been noticed:

- Inappropriate composition of bank boards or lack of domain expertise: A large number of banks were found not to have had adequate expertise in the financial sector on their boards. As a result, there was inadequate focus on issues of risk management. Citibank, for instance, had a former spook from the CIA on its audit committee. Lehman Brothers had a theater impresario as a member of its risk management committee.
- Lack of engagement between managers of funds that were invested in banks and the boards of banks. This point was made by the Walker Committee in the United Kingdom which was specifically tasked with looking into issues of governance thrown up by the financial crisis.[7] Fund managers do not engage actively because total equity shareholding in banks has thus far tended to be 2 percent or less of total capital. Any investor would have a small portion of the 2 percent. Thus, the exposure of any investor to a bank is very small. Moreover, fund managers are typically more interested in short-term performance and they prefer to exit a given stock instead of making the effort to engage with management on ensuring long-term performance.[8]
- Bondholders and creditors to banks can exert considerable influence on bank boards given that bonds are a significant source of funds for banks. In practice, they do not do so as they are aware of the implicit taxpayer guarantee that is available to them.[9]
- Remuneration policies for managers did not properly align reward with long-term performance.

Governance is thus largely left to boards of directors. Several committees have asked banks to give more importance to getting the right people on their boards, ensuring that independent directors are given proper training, induction, and exposure to the banks' business. The Walker

Committee recommended that independent directors be expected to devote 30 to 36 days to their boards.

How do we ensure that boards are effective? We need to be first clear about how boards are constituted. Individuals are invited on to boards as independent directors at the instance or with the concurrence of the CEO. For the most part, these are people the CEO has known or is comfortable with. They may not necessarily be persons with the requisite domain expertise or the ability to challenge the CEO.

In the United Kingdom, the Financial Services Authority (which regulated banks until bank regulation was moved back to the Bank of England after the crisis) had the practice of interviewing candidates for the boards of banks and other financial institutions in the FTSE-100, a widely tracked stock market index. Candidates found unsuitable were rejected. However, this is not a practice that is widely followed by regulators in general. The appointment of board members is left entirely to the boards themselves, subject to candidates meeting "fit and proper" criteria laid down by the regulator.

One of the biggest failures in the 2007 crisis was that of the Royal Bank of Scotland (RBS) in the United Kingdom. RBS had a set of good people with the necessary expertise on its board. It followed all the processes laid down for boards by various regulators. The chairman conducted the meetings professionally. In other words, the RBS board ticked all the right boxes. Yet, it could not prevent the failure of the bank. This shows that it is not enough to get the composition of boards right. A lot more needs to be done to improve governance.

The UK Parliamentary Commission on Banking set out four themes on which improvement is required:[10]

- Ensuring there is adequate challenge within boards;
- Ensuring personal responsibility of board members;
- Ensuring that boards do not remain willfully ignorant of what is happening at the banks; and
- Putting in place norms that take into account the fact that banks, unlike other companies, have a very small amount of equity capital.

Let us take up each one of these themes in turn.

Ensuring Adequate Challenge

How do we ensure that there is adequate challenge within boards? Domain expertise alone does not ensure challenge. Nor does diversity in skills or gender diversity, however useful these are. Boards lack adequate challenge because there is not enough diversity in selection of board members.

On paper, the selection of independent directors is done by a Nomination Committee comprising independent directors on the board. In practice, as mentioned earlier, independent directors are chosen in consultation with the CEO. It is rare for a board to select an individual whom the CEO is not comfortable with. There is a natural tendency to choose "people like us"—directors who have the same social background, frequent the same clubs and drawn from the same professional groups, say, corporate executives, retired bureaucrats, and former regulators.

Shareholders have little say in the selection of directors—the vote on director appointments is mostly an empty ritual. One way to address this problem is to allow large shareholders a say in the appointment of independent directors. The UK Parliamentary Commission report mentions that this system has been very effective in Scandinavian countries.[11] It is also worth exploring the possibility of having a representative of employees on the board. This happens in public sector banks in India.

The newly elected Prime Minister of UK, Theresa May, has thrown her weight behind the idea of having an employee representative on the boards of companies. "I want to see changes in the way that big business is governed. The people who run big businesses are supposed to be accountable to outsiders," May said. "In practice, they are drawn from the same narrow social and professional circles as the executive team."[12]

A good starting point would be to ensure that the full slate of independent directors on a bank board is not chosen by the board itself–we should allow various stakeholders, such as institutional investors, retail investors, big lenders, and others to appoint their nominees to the board. A suggestion made by the UK Parliamentary Commission, namely, that large-sized banks be required to advertise these positions, is also worth considering.

Ensuring Personal Responsibility

The UK Parliamentary Commission has proposed a Senior Persons regime for the board and top management whereby the responsibilities of the concerned persons will be made explicit.[13] It would like chairmen of boards to be responsible for promoting a free exchange of views and challenge within the board. It also wants chairmen to meet the chairmen of various subcommittees annually and it endorses the Walker Committee's proposal that chairmen should commit two-thirds of their time to their boards. It recommends that chairmen of financial institutions not hold any other large commercial nonexecutive or executive positions.

It also posits the senior independent director as an independent check on both the chairman and the CEO. It would like the senior independent director to review the performance of the chairman annually and also brief the regulators on the performance of the chairman. It would also like independent directors to use their powers to obtain professional advice, both internally and externally.

These are all unexceptionable recommendations. However, they leave answered one important question: Who is to enforce accountability in respect of each recommendation and what are the penalties for noncompliance?

Ensuring That Boards Do Not Remain Willfully Ignorant

There are a number of steps that boards can take to ensure that they are not kept out of the loop. Some of these steps have already been taken by banks or regulators. One, the chief risk officer (CRO) must report not just to the CEO but also to the independent director who heads the Risk Management Committee of the board. Decisions on removal of the CRO or remuneration of the CEO should not be taken without the approval of the chairman of the Risk Management Committee.

Similar measures can be applied to the head of compliance. It should also be the board's responsibility to put in place an effective policy on whistleblowing and to ensure that whistle blowers receive all necessary protection. These are some of the channels through which vital information can be accessed by the board.

Norms That Take into Account the Special Character of Banks

The UK Parliamentary Commission felt that, in addition to the steps outlined previously, banks had to make a special effort to change their culture and standards of behavior. While companies everywhere have an obligation to do so, the requirement is especially acute in the case of banks for the simple reason that banks are more prone to failure than the typical firm.

The Commission, however, was quick to acknowledge that a major cultural change in banking would take years to happen. It also noted that this had little to do with want of codes of conduct or declarations of intent—there was no dearth of these at banks that had failed. What was missing was a willingness to adhere to codes that existed.

Banks could take some concrete steps to improve their culture. One is to ensure that financial incentives do not work in an opposite direction to codes of conduct. The other is gender diversity, both at the board level and on the trading floor.[14]

Again, these are useful recommendations. However, it should be clear that governance at banks can improve only when boards are more effective. And board effectiveness cannot improve a great deal until the process of selection of independent directors changes drastically.

Changes in Remuneration Policy
for Bank Executives

There is a widespread perception that faulty remuneration policies were a contributory factor in the crisis. Remuneration policies before the crisis, it is believed, did not adequately align reward with risk, that is, rewards did not factor in the long-term risks involved in policies or strategies and thus ended up incentivizing short-term performance.

Firms such as Bear Stearns and Lehman Brothers produced some of their best performance in terms of return on equity in 2006. Top management was handsomely compensated. Two years later, the firms were gone. This is because of a fatal flaw in the way bankers were paid before the crisis.

Pay was related to performance defined as return on equity. It is possible to increase return on equity by increasing leverage, that is, by taking more risk. Thus, the key metric used to reward performance in banking created incentives for taking higher and higher risks.

In general, in the presence of high levels of debt, shareholders and managers both have every incentive to take risky bets. If the gambles they take work out, they stand to gain enormously. If they don't, it is the holders of debt who will pick up the losses. It's what we referred to in Chapter 2 as a heads-I-win-tails-you-lose philosophy.

Knowing this, providers of debt will not lend beyond a point. In banking, however, there is a crucial difference. Providers of debt know they will be bailed out by tax payers, so they are willing to provide more debt than they would in other cases. Linking rewards to return on equity thus encourages bankers to increase leverage and, having increased leverage, to indulge in risky bets.

There is also evidence that pay in banking has not fallen subsequent to 2007 despite losses or lower profit. In United Kingdom, for instance, total pay, that is, fixed pay plus variable pay, did not fall at the leading banks between 2007 and 2012. Since the number of employees went down in this period, average pay rose during this period. While variable pay was lower, banks moved to increase fixed pay thus keeping total pay unchanged. The UK Parliamentary Commission noted:[15]

> Rewards have been paid for failure. They are unjustified. Although the banks and those who speak for them are keen to present evidence that bonuses have fallen, fixed pay has risen, offsetting some of the effect of this fall. The result is that overall levels of remuneration in banking have largely been maintained. Aggregate pay levels of senior bankers have also been unjustified…. These elevated levels of remuneration are particularly unacceptable when banks are complaining of an inability to lend owing to the need to preserve capital and are also attempting to justify rises in charges for consumers.

Changing the basis for rewards in banking is crucial to ensuring that incentives for excessive risk-taking do not obtain. There are three reforms that are required.

First, we need to reduce the level of leverage. We have seen that high leverage produces incentives for managers to take risky bets. Reducing leverage would serve to reduce such incentives. Basel III, we have noted, is only the most modest of starts toward reduction in leverage. Leverage needs to fall a great deal more.

Second, we need to address the "too-big-to-fail" problem. When banks become large and their failure imposes costs on the economy, they will not be allowed to fail. This creates incentives for managers to take excessive risks. How to tackle this problem is addressed in Chapter 4.

Third, we need to change the structure of compensation itself. Regulators have sought to address three crucial elements of the structure of the compensation:

- The proportion of variable pay: It is accepted that some proportion of variable pay in total compensation is desirable. The question is what the appropriate proportion might be. In the United Kingdom, since 2010, variable pay of 50 percent has been thought desirable.[16] The European Union's position is that a ceiling on variable pay is desirable—in other words, too much of variable pay is as bad as not having variable pay at all. Too much of variable pay linked to performance leads bankers to take excessive risks and hence must be contained.

   In the European Union, regulators have decided that the ratio of fixed pay to variable pay can be only 1:1. With the approval of shareholders, this can rise to 1:2. Under current proposals, these ceilings will kick in from January, 2017.[17]

- Deferral of variable pay: Risks in banking take fairly long to show up. If bad loans have been made for long-duration projects, this will become known only after several years. It is the same with mis-selling insurance. Consumers wake up and protest after they have been led down the garden path for a while.

   Under rules that came into force in 2011, the European Union requires banks with assets of more than £15 billion to defer at least 40 percent of the variable remuneration award or 60 percent where the total variable pay is more than £500,000. It also stipulates a minimum deferral period of three to five years. Lastly, the payout should be in equal tranches.

   In the United Kingdom and the United States, regulators are averse to setting limits on variable pay. They would prefer to focus on longer periods of deferral. The United Kingdom, for instance, is considering deferral of bonus for up to 7 years and, perhaps, even 10 years. In addition, regulators in both countries are keen on "clawback" provisions that would require banks to deduct from bonuses due if the bankers have inflicted losses on the banks or violated regulations. The United States has proposed deferrals of 60 percent of incentive-based pay for at least four years. It also intends clawback of bonuses for up to seven years if bankers are found to have engaged in misconduct or caused losses to the bank.[18]

• Using the right metrics to reward bankers: We have seen that linking bankers' rewards to return on equity is flawed—it encourages bankers to increase leverage and exposes banks to greater risk. Following the crisis, regulators want banks to use a different set of metrics to reward bankers.

Rewards must be linked to risk-adjusted return on equity—this would be capture not just the return produced but the risk taken in doing so and the capital required for the purpose. There is also a sense that bankers' rewards must be linked to nonfinancial measures such as the overall financial soundness of the bank (measured by capital adequacy, the level of nonperforming assets, etc.), customer satisfaction, and compliance with regulation.

Macroprudential Regulation

The general buildup of debt and the creation of a housing bubble, we saw in the previous chapter, was one of the most important causes of the financial crisis of 2007. There was no mechanism by which the debt buildup and the associated bubble could be tracked and responded to.

The monetary authority in various economies (the Bank of England in the United Kingdom and the Federal Reserve in the United States) focused on inflation and did not think it necessary or appropriate to respond to increases in asset prices. To a large extent, this reflected the perception that it was hard for the monetary authority to determine whether an increase in asset prices was a bubble or whether it reflected conditions in the real economy such as higher growth or low interest rates.

The regulatory authorities focused on individual institutions and were not in the business of monitoring aggregates, such as the total expansion of credit, the overall liquidity mismatches in the system or the leverage ratio in the system as a whole. Yet, we know that when instability builds up in the system as a whole, individual institutions are bound to be impacted.

Similarly, we need to monitor the exposure of the financial system to systemically important financial institutions (SIFIs). These could be direct exposures to the SIFI or exposures to assets that the SIFI has on its balance sheet. Banks could have subsidiaries in the insurance, mutual fund, private equity, brokerage, and other areas. The bank regulator may not have access to information on risks building up in these other areas to which banks are exposed.

There has been recognition since the financial crisis that we need to have macroprudential regulation, that is, a mechanism by which aggregate risks in the system are monitored and communicated to the regulatory authority and regulatory tools are used to reduce risk at the level of institutions. The United Kingdom has set up a Financial Policy Committee under the Bank of England to perform this role. The United States has set up a Financial Stability Oversight Council to do so. Similar bodies have sprung up in other countries.

A number of tools can be brought into play to contain excessive buildup of risks in the system:[19]

- Seeking activation of the countercyclical capital buffers of the sort proposed under Basel III: When there's a boom, the capital requirements are raised. (Under recessionary conditions, capital requirements are lowered.) Such measures may not dampen the boom. However, it makes banks better equipped to handle the bust whenever it happens.
- Variation in sectoral or product risk weights: The regulator may increase the risk weights for particular sectors such as real estate or for products such as credit cards if lending to these sectors is seen to be growing at an unhealthy pace.
- Dynamic provisioning: In good times, banks are required to set aside provisions for bad loans in addition to those

prescribed by regulatory norms so that they are better placed
to absorb losses in a downturn. Spain, Chile, Colombia,
Peru, and Uruguay are among those who have introduced a
dynamic provisioning regime.

- Loan-to-value ratios: It is possible to dampen lending to the
  real estate sector by specifying a suitably high loan-to-value
  ratio for banks, that is, the portion of the value of a property
  that can be financed through a loan.
- Measures targeting foreign currency exposures of companies:
  When companies take out foreign currency loans, any appreciation in the foreign currency translates into a credit risk for
  the lender. If there is a perception that a foreign currency or
  currencies are likely to appreciate with respect to the domestic
  currency, limits on foreign currency exposures of corporates
  can be introduced.
- Liquidity requirements: When liquidity is freely available, it
  may make sense to get banks to build up a buffer of liquid
  assets that can be drawn up when liquidity dries up. New
  Zealand and Korea have used such measures.
- Closer monitoring of SIFIs: The risks caused by SIFIs have
  emerged center stage consequent to the financial crisis. They
  will be subject to extra capital requirements under Basel III.
  However, some additional measures may be required to limit
  the risks arising from failure of such institutions. One would
  be to require extra capital of institutions exposed to SIFIs.
  Another would to require greater transparency in exposures to
  SIFIs, including derivative exposures.

Macroprudential regulation also requires cooperation at the international level. This is because monetary policies or an expansion in liquidity
in one country can spill over into other countries in an era in which most
economies are substantially open. Cooperation is also required because
financial institutions and markets are international and cannot be monitored or regulated at the national level alone.

In 2010, the European Union has set up the European Systemic
Risk Board to oversee risk in the Union. It is hosted and supported by

the European Central Bank (ECB) and includes members of the ECB, national central banks, and supervisory authorities of the EU states and the European Commission. At the international level, the Financial Stability Board was set up in 2009 as a successor to the Financial Stability Forum. The Board, which is based in Basel, includes members of the G-20 countries, Financial Stability Forum members and the European Commission.

Macroprudential regulation does entail costs. It could mean limiting the possibilities of growth in order to head off asset bubbles. Increasing levels of stability and liquidity in the system increases the cost of credit. Thus, macroprudential regulation involves a trade-off between stability and efficiency in the financial system.

Evaluating the Role of Rating Agencies

Rating agencies, we have seen in Chapter 3, played a role in bringing about the financial crisis. It was the high ratings accorded to securitized mortgage products that created an enormous appetite for these and left banks and others heavily exposed to them.

Much of the debate on rating agencies since has focused on three aspects of their functioning.[20] First, regulatory agencies for the financial markets (such as SEC) and banks have made it mandatory for investment funds and banks to obtain ratings while making investments. Some mutual funds have internal rules that mandate that investment be made only in instruments that have been rated investment grade. This gives rating agencies a huge captive market for their services.

Second, the rating agencies have taken the position that they are independent assessors of credit risk and hence immune to legal challenge on the basis of their "free speech rights." The courts have tended to uphold this view although, after the financial crisis, the Justice Department managed to arrive at a $1.4 billion settlement with Standard & Poor's regarded inflated ratings issued by it prior to the crisis.

Third, there is a conflict of interest inherent in ratings being paid for by the issuer. There are obvious incentives for rating agencies to please issuers by giving them favorable ratings in the interest of getting more business.

Part of the answer to the first problem would seem to be to create more rating agencies. In the United States, the Credit Rating Agency Reform Act of 2006 sought to do so by having more Nationally Recognized Statistical Rating Organizations (NRSROs) added to the three that obtained at the time. There are nine NRSROs in the United States but around 97 percent of the business still goes to the top three. It has not been possible to inject meaningful competition into the business in the United States or elsewhere. There is also the danger that, with too many agencies competing for business, it may become easier for issuers to shop around for the agency that gives the best rating. This would have the effect of lowering rating standards.

As for conflicts of interest, some solutions have been proposed. One is to have investors pay the agencies instead of the issuers of securities. This approach is, however, exposed to the free rider problem—if one investor pays for ratings and invests in a security, other investors would get to know of the investment and do likewise without having to pay for the ratings.

A solution proposed is to have the SEC select randomly from among the agencies for a given security. But if this is done, rating agencies will have no incentive to hire good people and do the best job they can. On the other hand, they will have incentives to cut costs and offer the bare minimum. This again would not serve the purpose that ratings are intended to do, which is provide investors an accurate idea of how good a given security is.

A variant of this idea is to have stock exchanges pay for ratings by collecting a cess from those who list securities on the exchanges and use the funds to pay the rating agencies. But this does not solve the problem mentioned above: How to pick a rating agency in a given case?

One interesting solution proposed for the conflict of interest problem is to have the rating agencies have "skin in the game."[21] Let the rating agencies be paid in part by the securities they are rating. But this would require agencies to devote energy to managing investment which may not be part of their competence. Moreover, rating agencies may not be willing to invest in securities below a certain rating—in these cases, they would have to be paid entirely in cash.

Why not have a publicly owned rating agency run on a nonprofit basis? Well, there are the dangers of monopoly. There are also the risks of political interference in ratings that go with public ownership.

Lastly, we could consider not requiring securities to be rated. Investors could use market prices to determine their investment. However, market prices are volatile and it would be difficult for banks, for instance, to allocate capital based on market prices. Alternatively, investors and banks could use their own internal research for making decisions on securities.

In sum, the reform of rating agencies remains very much part of the unfinished agenda arising from the financial crisis. We cannot do without the agencies. At the same time, we have thus far been unable to find ways to significantly address shortcomings in the way they have functioned.

Norms for Securitization

There has been something of a backlash against securitization consequent to the crisis. This is because investment by banks and financial institutions in securitized products left them exposed to assets that turned out to be illiquid and not as free from risk as they had supposed.

But this is not an argument against securitization *per se*. We have to make a distinction between relatively simple securitization products and complex ones. Simple securitization products are those based on clear cash flows, for instance, the securitization of credit card receivables or automobile loans. During the financial crisis, problems arose on account of complex securitization products, that is, products whose risks were not clear and hence could not be accurately rated.

Regulators in the United States and Europe have responded in broadly similar ways to the problems with securitization that were highlighted by the financial crisis. One part has to do with rating agencies—this has been covered in the preceding. The other parts are: improving disclosure, risk-retention on the part of originators, and higher capital requirements for certain securitization transactions.[22]

   i. Disclosure:

     In the United States, the Dodd Frank Act requires disclosure of information on the financial assets backing each class of asset-backed securities. This requirement will need to be translated into rules by the SEC.

In the European Union, the effort is to incentivize simple, transparent, and standardized (STS) securitization. Simplicity is sought to be achieved by requiring the true sale of the underlying financial assets. Further, the assets must be homogeneous, creditworthy and not constituting already securitized financial assets.

The requirement of creditworthiness is worth emphasizing. Those seeking to sell securitized products must ensure that those from whom the assets have been sourced are solvent, not in default and do not have adverse credit history or low scores—factors that, we know, contributed to serious problems in securitized products in the financial crisis.

Standardization means that securitized products must not include derivative products other than those included for hedging interest rate and exchange rate risk. Under transparency requirements, the originator or sponsor must provide investors a cash flow model and also historical information on delinquency, default, and loss on comparable products. An independent, external party must verify a sample of the assets offered for securitization.

ii. Risk-retention: The Dodd Frank Act requires sponsors or originators to retain some portion of the securitized assets that they are selling or transferring to another party. For example, in the case of "nonqualified" residential mortgage assets, they are required to retain 5 percent of the credit risk involved. ("Nonqualified" mortgages are mortgages that do not satisfy the requirement of a Qualified Mortgage (QM) under rules framed by the Consumer Financial Protection Bureau in the United States. A QM mortgage gives the originator protection from lawsuits provide they meet certain conditions attached to such mortgages.)

The European Union has laid down a similar requirement. The motivation in having risk-retention is that originators will exercise some care in the quality of loans they originate. Whether 5 percent is an adequate level of risk-retention is, however, debatable.

iii. Higher capital charge: Under Basel II, banks could follow a Standardized Approach (SA) for computing capital charges (which was based on ratings given by external agencies) or an Internal Ratings-Based Approach, in which banks could use their own models for computing credit (subject to these models being validated by regulators).

The Basel II norms incentivized banks to acquire securitized products because the capital charges for securitized products were, in many cases, much lower than those for holding loans. If a bank held a mortgage loan (which is typically unrated), the risk weight applicable was 35 percent. If the same loan was converted into a AAA securitization tranche, the risk weight was 20 percent under the Standardized Ratings method and a mere 7 percent under the Internal Ratings-Based method.

Under Basel III, the SA is replaced by the Simplified Supervisory Formula Approach (SSFA). The Revised Ratings-Based Approach (RRBA), which replaces the Internatal Ratings Based (IRB) approach of Basel II, distinguishes between longer and shorter maturity of tranches and also increases the risk weights and leads to greater capital charges than the IRB approach in Basel II. The Backstop Credit Rating Approach (BCRA) is a fall-back approach and likewise leads to higher capital charges. Clearly, the intention in all these methods is to ensure is banks cannot reduce their capital charges merely by substituting loans with securitized products.

Without getting into the details of the approach, we can see in the following Table 3.2 that risk weights for lower tranches have been increased sharply. For instance, a tranche with a credit rating of AA carried a risk weight of 20 percent in the SA. Under SSFA, the risk weight shoot up to 567 percent. Under IRB, the same tranche had a risk weight of 8 percent. This rises to 67, 281, and 1,250 percent under RRBA (where the maturity is of one year), RRBA (with a maturity of three years) and BCRA respectively.

Addressing Global Imbalances and Global Regulation

As mentioned in Chapter 2, there is a sense that global imbalances contributed to the financial crisis. However, this is not an outcome that was clearly foreseen by many economists. Indeed, prior to the crisis, there were three distinct views on global imbalances.[23]

Table 3.2 *Illustrative calculations of bank capital requirements under Basel II and the new BCBS proposals (U.S. high-quality mortgage deal) 1/2/ (in percent)*

Tranche	Credit rating	Tranche thickness	Basel II				BCBS proposals							
			SA		IRB		SSFA		RRBA (maturity=1) 3/		RRBA (maturity=5) 3/		BCRA	
			RW	4/ CCR	RW	4/ CCR	RW	4/ CCR	RW	4/ CCR	RW	4/ CCR	RW	4/ CCR
A1	AAA	92.95	20	1.49	7	0.52	20	1.49	20	1.49	49	3.64	50	3.72
B1	AA	2.65	20	0.04	8	0.02	567	1.20	67	0.14	281	0.60	1,250	2.65
B2	A	1.40	50	0.06	12	0.01	1,217	1.36	220	0.25	422	0.47	1,250	1.40
B3	BBB	1.15	100	0.09	60	0.06	1,250	1.15	609	0.56	707	0.65	1,250	1.15
B4	BB	0.80	350	0.22	425	0.27	1,250	0.80	1,181	0.76	1,250	0.80	1,250	0.80
B5	NR	1.05	1,250	1.05	1,250	1.05	1,250	1.05	1,250	1.05	1,250	1.05	1,250	1.05
Weighted average risk-weight			37		24		88		53		90		135	

Total capital charge ($mn) on $100mn deal	2.95	1.93	7.05	4.24	7.21	10.77
Multiple of capital charge on deal vis-à-vis if loans held on balance sheet	0.74	0.48	1.76	1.06	1.80	2.69

Source: Securitization: Lessons learned and the road ahead: Miguel Segoviano, Bradley Jones, Peter Lindner, and Johannes Blankenheim, IMF Working Paper WP/13/255.

Glossary: SA: Standardized Approach; IRB: Internal Ratings-Based Approach; SSFA: Simplified Supervisory Formula Approach; RRBA: Revised Ratings-Based Approach; BCRA: Backstop Concentration Ratio Approach.

1/ A $100 million transaction involving high-quality U.S. mortgages is assumed.

2/ The risk weight of the underlying loans is set at 50 percent, implying a total capital charge for the underlying loans of 4 percent (i.e., 50 of 8 percent), or $4 million.

3/ At origination, mortgages will usually have a maturity closer to five years than to one year. The RRBA formula resulting in the higher risk weights and capital charges would therefore apply.

4/ Contribution to Capital Requirement (CCR) denotes the U.S. dollar amount that each tranche contributes to the capital requirement of the whole deal, based on a $100 million securitization.

One view, propounded by former Fed Chairman Ben Bernanke, was that global imbalances were the result of a "saving glut" in some emerging markets such as China and a saving deficit in countries such as the United States. A "saving glut" arose from several factors. Household saving was high in countries such as China. Many emerging markets wanted to accumulate currency reserves as insurance against a balance of payments crisis. Oil producing countries had large surpluses on account of oil prices which they wanted to park in U.S. securities. Many advanced economies had a saving deficit because of the factors such as an ageing population and a scarcity of investment opportunities.

Large current account surpluses in some countries were the obverse side of large capital account outflows. Large current account deficits were the obverse side of large capital inflows. In Bernanke's scheme of things, there was nothing unstable about this arrangement. Indeed, confidence in the dollar rendered such flows stable.

Others believed that global imbalances were a part of "Bretton Woods-II," a sequel to Bretton Woods-I. The latter was the international exchange rate system which was based on the gold standard (whereby the price of gold in dollar terms was fixed). The gold standard had been replaced by the dollar as the anchor of stability in the international financial system. It was natural for capital surpluses everywhere to be invested in dollar-denominated government securities.

A third view on global imbalances, which contradicted the first two, was that it was inherently unstable. One group of countries persistently produced more goods than it needed and another was absorbing more goods than it produced. As the United States depended more and more on others to finance its consumption, one day the level of U.S. debt would become unsustainable and cause the dollar to collapse, thus triggering a major currency crisis.

As it turned out, this is not how the collapse came about—the dollar did not collapse. Instead, asset prices in the United States started soaring. Once the asset bubble was pricked, American households could not service their debt and this caused a collapse of the banking system. Global imbalances thus contributed to the crisis in a way that was not anticipated by many economists.

How do we rectify global imbalances? We need current account deficit countries to reduce spending and surplus countries to increase spending. The surplus countries need to let their currencies appreciate and the deficit countries rein in monetary and fiscal policy in order to control spending. Both are easier said than done. For the deficit countries to control spending is especially difficult when many face weak growth or even recession.

At the G-20 Seoul summit of 2011, leaders of these countries committed themselves to maintain current imbalances within range of 4 percent of GDP. But we do not have a mechanism to enforce such commitments. We must depend on the good sense of each individual country to behave well.

As long as the dollar remains the reserve currency, the problem of global imbalances will remain. Since the dollar is the reserve currency, the United States has no incentives to contain its current account deficit. It can print as many dollars as it like to finance its deficits. To put it differently, there will always be enough capital inflows into the dollar to finance America's current deficits. The United States is, in some sense, predisposed toward a large current account deficit as it is the first choice of countries seeking to park their reserves, has the deepest capital markets, and enjoys the world's confidence as its only superpower.[24]

The fundamental answer thus is to move to a reserve currency other than the dollar—say, the Special Drawing Rights issued by the IMF. Such a move would transform the IMF into a global central bank. While this has been an item on the agenda for global economic reform for quite some time, there is little prospect of its becoming a reality in the near future. We must be reconciled to foreign money flooding into the United States. The more realistic response would be to better police the U.S. financial system and ensure that it does not collapse.

Containing macroeconomic imbalances also requires coordination of a range of policies on macroeconomic goals among nations. The Stiglitz Commission, constituted by the UN, was of the view that the forum best suited for the purpose was the UN. It also felt that agencies such as the IMF and the World Bank had their own institutional foci and that, therefore, it would be useful to create an "overarching inclusive body" that would be responsible for global economic governance.[25]

To begin with, an Intergovernmental Panel could be set up for the assessment and monitoring of systemic risks in the global economy. The Panel would comprise experts from advanced economies as well as emerging and economies and from all continents. The institution could be modeled on the Intergovernmental Panel on Climate Change (IPCC) which has proved successful. The Panel would serve as an advisory body to the UN, the Bretton Woods institutions and other institutions dealing with economic, financial, and social issues.

Over the long term, the Stiglitz Commission recommends the creation of a Global Economic Coordination Council at a level equivalent with the UN General Assembly and the Security Council. The proposed Council would provide leadership on a range of economic issues while taking into account social and economic factors. The intergovernmental Panel would play a role in defining the mandate, working mechanisms, composition, and the interaction of the Council with the UN system. Once the Council is set up, the Intergovernmental Panel would continue to provide advice to it.

The Stiglitz Commission would also like the IMF, the World Bank, and other multilateral institutions to play an active role in promoting economic development and stability. However, it notes:

> The severe shortcomings in the mandate, policies, resources, and governance of these institutions have impaired their ability to take adequate actions to prevent and respond to the crisis and have also had a negative impact on their mandate to promote sustainable development. The ability of the IMF to safeguard the stability of the global economy has been undermined by the vastly greater resources and volatility of globally integrated private financial institutions. Uncoordinated national policy responses have made the task it faces all the more difficult.
>
> The effectiveness and credibility of the Bretton Woods Institutions have been adversely affected by deficiencies in governance (including their skewed voting structures and nondemocratic

processes of choosing their heads), the checkered record of their forecasting, policy, and other recommendations, including the onerous conditionalities they have imposed on borrowing countries and their tendency to proffer pro-cyclical rather than counter-cyclical policy advice. Major reforms are thus necessary.[26]

Greater coordination is also required in the regulation and supervision of major global banks with cross-border operations. The failure of Lehman Brothers showed that when a large bank fails in a particular country, the effect is felt in other countries where the bank has operations even if those other operations are through independent subsidiaries. This is because a loss of confidence in a bank in, say, the home country finds an echo in other countries in which it operates. It is important, therefore, for regulators and supervisors to coordinate their actions in order to reduce the likelihood of cross-border failures and the impact these have.

One obvious need is for greater exchange of information among supervisors. Toward this end, the Financial Stability Forum has proposed a College of Supervisors that would monitor major cross-border financial institutions. The FSF has also set up a working group that has defined how supervisors and monetary authorities might cooperate under crisis conditions.

However, the Turner Review points out that there are limitations to what international cooperation can achieve when fiscal support for failed banks is entirely the responsibility of national governments. For instance, the failure of large U.S. banks has global consequences but it was left to the U.S. government to provide fiscal support to these banks.[27] The Turner Review believes that, without a more unified approach to global supervision and even fiscal support, coordination through colleges of supervisors would not help beyond a point.

Are the regulatory changes adequate? Do they significantly reduce the probability of another major financial crisis? We think not. The too-big-to-fail problem is yet to be satisfactorily addressed. Moreover, reducing the prospects of another financial crisis may require radical approaches that go well beyond the regulations initiated so far. We explore these topics in Chapters 4 and 5.

Summary

Several changes in regulation have happened in response to the financial crisis. Capital requirements for banks have been increased. Stringent norms for liquidity have been introduced. Some steps have been taken to improve governance at banks. Regulators have moved to ensure that executive pay is linked to long-term performance. Macroprudential regulation, which is the monitoring of aggregate risks in the system, has been set in motion. Norms for securitization of assets have been tightened. The role of rating agencies and global imbalances, however, are two areas where action thus far has been inadequate.

As we will see in Chapters 4 and 5, these measures may not suffice to significantly reduce the probability of a financial crisis–we need initiatives that go well beyond them.

CHAPTER 4

Addressing the Too-Big-To-Fail Problem

Trend Toward Bigness in Banking

Banks have been getting bigger and bigger and this is especially true of large banks. An IMF study documents the main trends:[1]

- The balance sheet of the world's six largest banks doubled and, in some cases, quadrupled in the 10 years preceding the financial crisis.
- The scope of banks' activities has increased. Banks have moved away from the traditional business of making loans into activities such as proprietary trading, market-marking, origination and holding of securitized debt, security dealing and custodial services, and the provision of services such as advisory and hedging to customers. This is reflected in a fall in the loan to assets ratio and an increase in noninterest income to total income. These trends are especially pronounced in the case of large banks.
- Large banks hold less capital than small banks, whether measured by capital to risk-weighted assets or a simple leverage ratio (equity to total assets).
- Large banks also have less stable funding compared to small banks, measured by the ratio of deposits to total liabilities.
- Large banks are organizationally more complex. Complexity is measured by the number of subsidiaries a bank has.

The IMF paper also finds that among large banks, the four dimensions—low capital, stability of funding, share of market-based activities, and organizational complexity—are correlated. There must be reasons, therefore, for banks to get larger while having these features.

Another study documents the increase in size of American banks.[2] The study looked at the 11 banks judged to be too-big-to-fail (TBTF) in 1984. In 1983, these 11 banks accounted for $2 trillion in assets and nearly 30 percent of the total assets of the banking system. By 2014, only 4 out of the 11 banks remained, with 5 of the original banks becoming part of one bank, JP Morgan Chase. The 4 banks that remained had total assets of over $13 trillion and accounted for 30.3 percent of total bank assets (Table 4.1). Citibank is nearly 13 times what it was 30 years ago, Bank of America 14 times, and Wells Fargo Bank 6 times.

Table 4.1 Growth in U.S. banks' size in 1983–2014

Bank	Assets at end-1983 ($ millions)	% of total bank assets	Assets at end-2014 ($ millions)	% increase	% of total Bank
Citibank	$1,04,392	5.2	$13,53,237	1196%	9.8
Bank of America	$1,04,085	5.2	$14,57,856	1301%	10.5
Chase Manhattan Bank	$72,956	3.6	NA		
Morgan Guaranty Trust	$54,368	2.7	NA		
Manufacturers Hanover Trust	$54,321	2.7	NA		
Chemical Bank	$45,956	2.3	NA		
Continental Illinois National Bank & Trust	$39,811	2	NA		
Bankers Trust	$36,949	1.8	$60,464	64%	0.004
Security Pacific National Bank	$34,329	1.7	NA		
First National Bank of Chicago	$33,505	1.7	NA		
Wells Fargo Bank	$23,390	1.2	$13,88,274	5835%	10
Total commercial bank assets	$20,18,593	29.9	13,854,733		30.3

Source: James R. Barth Moutusi Sau (2014).

Table 4.2 Holding companies of remaining four original too-big-to-fail banks, year-end 2013

Bank holding company	BHC's assets ($ millions)	% of total BHC assets
JP Morgan Chase & Co.	$24,76,986	14.6
Bank of America Corp.	$21,52,533	12.7
Citigroup Inc.	$18,94,736	11.2
Wells Fargo & Co.	$15,46,707	9.1
Total bank holding company assets	$1,69,11,000	47.7

Source: James R. Barth and Moutusi Sau (2014).

Banks are part of larger Bank Holding Companies (BHCs). Table 4.2 tells us how big the four BHCs of 1983 that remain in 2014 are in relation to the banking system. They account for 47.7 percent of all BHC assets.

Banks have also grown big in relation to the economy. Assets of U.S. banks, which had for long been a quarter of the GDP, rose to 100 percent of GDP by the time of the crisis. In the United Kingdom, bank assets were 500 percent of GDP. In Ireland, Switzerland, and Iceland, they were even bigger.[3] The world's top 20 banks account for almost 40 percent of worldwide banking assets.[4] The assets of the top 10 banks in the United States amount to over 60 percent of GDP; in the United Kingdom, the same figure is 450 percent of GDP.[5]

The failure of these entities thus poses serious risks to the economy at large.

Why Banks Are Getting Bigger?

As we have noted several times earlier, banks that are very big are not allowed to fail. That is because their failure spells damage to the economy at large. Banks are crucial to the payments system. For instance, cheques issued against deposits of a failed bank will not go through. This can create havoc to those to whom payments are due.

Moreover, the bank's borrowers will lose access to valuable finance. Confidence among depositors and creditors in general will be shaken and this could lead to panic spreading in the banking system. A large bank's failure is like the wake created by a giant ship sinking—within a wide area surrounding the ship, everything gets sucked in.

The problem is not just with banks that are large in terms of assets. Banks to which other important financial institutions are connected also qualify for rescue. So do nonbanks that are central to the financial system in one way or another. While TBTF is convenient journalistic shorthand, the more accurate way to characterize the problem is to look at systemically important financial institutions (SIFIs). It goes without saying, however, that banks that are very large would generally qualify as SIFIs and constitute a large chunk of the problem.

There are thus clear incentives for banks (and other financial institutions) to grow bigger. Knowing that they will not be allowed to fail, they can take big risks. Again, as we noted in an earlier chapter, if the gambles work out, there are enormous rewards for shareholders and managers. If they don't, tax payer money will be used to save the banks.

Given that equity is only a small proportion of overall assets, shareholders are happy to go along with banks taking large risks. Bondholders know they will be bailed out, so they too will go along. They will not demand the higher premium that goes with higher risk. There is thus an implicit subsidy to being a big bank—the costs of borrowing don't quite reflect the risk of failure, given the high probability that the bank will not be allowed to fail.

Depositors too lack the incentives to monitor SIFIs closely as they feel secure in the knowledge that they will be taken care of if the bank fails. The UK provided a vivid illustration of this during the last financial crisis: UK local authorities had deposits of nearly a billion dollars with Icelandic banks in 2008 and they continued to invest despite clear signs of failure.[6]

A second motivation for banks to grow bigger is that there are scale economies—that is, the unit cost of operations falls with size. For instance, the high fixed costs that go with information technology are better absorbed by a large institution. Third, there could be economies of scope, that is, the costs of combining two activities could be less than the sum of the costs of each individual activity. This happens because of synergies in using a set of inputs to produce multiple outputs. Fourth, there could be benefits to large banks arising from diversification and the resultant lowering of risk.

Last, there's a motivation that applies to firms in general. It has to do with what is called "managerial empire-building." It suits corporate executives to pursue growth because executive compensation is correlated with firm size and executives derive several private benefits from running a large firm.

We can now venture some explanations for why large banks exhibit in a pronounced form some of the features we outlined at the beginning of the chapter. Because size allows diversification and helps lower risk, large banks can afford to have lower capital and engage in market-based activities that are riskier than traditional lending. Market-based activities could result in higher leverage and unstable funding because securities can be used as collateral for raising funds in the repo market.

Several studies exist on economies of scope and scale in banking. Early studies found evidence of economies of scale for banks up to the range of $10–20 billion but not thereafter. On economies of scope, there is weak evidence that cost synergies exist either among deposits, loans, and other traditional banking products or between balance sheet and off-balance sheets items.[7]

More recent studies which used data from 2000s have found evidence of economies of scale at much higher sizes of assets. One study found scale economies for banks with assets up to $1 trillion and another for assets up to around $1.5 trillion. Yet another study, using data on banks with assets in excess of $100 billion, not only found scale-economies but argued that these may increase with bank size.[8]

These studies appear to suggest that size does help—the bigger, the better. However, these studies are based on estimates of banks' funding costs. These estimates do not take into account the implicit subsidy that goes with being TBTF. (We will elaborate on the implicit subsidy later.) What happens once this subsidy is removed and funding costs go up? One study found that the benefits of the economies of scale get reduced. After adjusting for the subsidy, it found that beyond $100 billion, there is no evidence of economies of scale.

Another study, however, comes to quite opposite conclusions. It finds that it is technology that is the source of scale economies, not the implicit subsidy. Hence, reducing the size of banks by scaling back their mix of products and services would significantly raise the costs of production. In other words, breaking up large banks into smaller ones would undermine the competitiveness of U.S. banks.[9]

The evidence on scale economies is thus inconclusive. However, even if we were to concede that size leads to reduction in costs, we would have to factor in diseconomies arising from greater complexity. The benefits of economies of scale could well be offset by growing complexity (or what might be called "diseconomies of scale").

Beyond a certain size, it becomes difficult to manage assets because of the sheer demands that size and complexity make on top management attention. For management to keep track of the various parts of the bank is a challenge. This would be especially true of banks that are spread across the globe and are engaged in a wide range of products and activities.

In other words, large size may make it difficult for management to manage risks and hence bigness could contribute to greater systemic risk. Policy makers, then, have to weigh the benefits of size against the costs in terms of systemic risk.

Here's a telling quote from a senior executive of Citigroup:[10]

> The complexity of the organization does provide us with a lot of challenge—it provides everybody with a lot of challenge—and the complexity and multiplicity of our technology systems mean that sometimes getting hold of information is burdensome and time-consuming. Having an organization such as Citi, with 250,000 employees, which has built up over a period of organic growth and acquisition, inevitably leads to quite a complex set of technologies.

Andrew Haldane, a former executive director with the Bank of England, illustrates the point by citing the instance of JP Morgan:[11]

> If anyone was viewed as having emerged successful from this crisis globally, it probably was JP Morgan; its risk management was seen as being best of breed, yet we had the London Whale incident, which suggests that a key part of that business was not being man-aged or overseen from a risk perspective in an effective way.... The evidence base is not encouraging about whether the biggest banks in the world can indeed manage themselves across the board.

If there are no benefits of scale or scope to be had beyond a certain size and if complexity becomes a problem, what drives the relentless drive among banks to get bigger? Well, as said earlier, it's clearly the knowledge that, once they are big enough to qualify as TBTF, they will not be allowed to fail.

We mentioned earlier the implicit subsidy that goes with being TBTF or SIFI. Without any subsidy, SIFIs would have to borrow at a certain interest rate. Thanks to the implicit subsidy, the cost of borrowing is lower. The difference between the two borrowing rates captures the implicit subsidy. The subsidy drives banks to grow bigger and bigger. And once banks become very big, managerial incentives get distorted in ways that sow the seeds for failure.

How large are the implicit subsidies? Several ways of measuring these have been attempted. One way to do so is to compare the "standalone" and "support" ratings issued to large banks.[12] The "standalone" rating is the agency's assessment of the probability of a bank's failure absent external support. The "support" rating is the probability of failure given government support. The difference between the two ratings thus gives the agency's assessment of the probability that the government will step in to save the bank.

For the 29 institutions that the FSB had judged to be SIFIs, the difference in the precrisis period averaged 1.3 notches (each notch represents a rating assigned by the agency). Over the period 2002–07, the implied annual subsidy to the world's largest banks averaged $70 billion per year using a ratings-based measure. This was roughly 50 percent of the average post-tax profits of these banks over the period.

By 2009, the difference in ratings had more than doubled to nearly three notches. The implied subsidy was now a staggering $700 billion. This was more than the average annual precrisis profits of these firms. It showed that "too-big-to-fail had had become hard-wired into the structure and pricing of the financial system."[13] In the United Kingdom, the value of the implicit subsidy has been estimated to be in the range of £10–50 billion.[14] In the major economies, the IMF estimated the cost of implicit subsidies at $200–300 billion in 2011.[15]

We are thus in an unenviable situation when it comes to managing the banking system. The implicit subsidies that go with size create incentives for banks to grow ever larger. However, it is not clear that growing bigger confers benefits in terms of either economies of scale or scope. Even where it does, we are not sure that the benefits outweigh the cost of higher systemic risk. In short, the financial system we have today seems geared to produce instability rather than stability

How do we address the problem of SIFIs? There are four broad approaches:

   i. Higher capital requirements for SIFIs
  ii. Mechanisms for orderly resolution in the event of failure
 iii. Limiting the scope of banks
 iv. Limiting the size of banks

In what follows, we consider each of these in turn.

Higher Capital for SIFIs

One way to discourage banks from getting bigger would be to impose a tax on size. Basel III, we noted, has proposed an additional capital charge of up to 2.5 percent for SIFIs.

Will such a tax be effective enough, meaning will it reduce the probability of failure of large banks and the losses in the financial system? We noted in Chapter 3 that leverage in banking remains far too high even after the higher capital requirements proposed by Basel III. We cited the contention that for banks to be much safer, we will need to move from the leverage ratio of 33:1 under Basel III to something like 4:1 or 5:1.

Still, it's worth assessing to what extent the systemic risk surcharge under Basel III will help. One study estimates the impact of the capital surcharge on the expected losses facing the 29 SIFIs identified by the Financial Stability Board.[16]

The study assumes that the base level of equity in the banks would be 7 percent as specified under Basel III and that a bank defaults on its obligations only when its capital is fully exhausted. It assumes that, in the event of default, banks suffer losses of around 30 percent on their assets. Without a surcharge, expected losses for the 29 SIFIs amount to around $200 billion per year. If the capital surcharge is 2.5 percent, expected losses fall by 60 percent. In order to reduce expected losses by 90 percent, a surcharge of over 7 percent would be needed.

The previous calculation assumes that default risks across banks are independent of each other. We know, however, that this is not true—in times of systemic crises, defaults tend to get correlated. Assuming a high degree of default correlation, the systemic loss rises to $750 billion. A capital surcharge of 2.5 percent reduces the loss to $350 billion, still a very large figure. To eliminate 90 percent of the loss, a surcharge of 15 percent is required, which is six times what is proposed under Basel III.

The study emphasizes that these are conservative estimates. If we were to relax some of the underlying assumptions (such as banks' defaulting only after their capital is exhausted), the losses turn out to be much bigger. The message is clear enough and it reinforces the contention of many critics of Basel III: The capital level proposed, including the systemic risk surcharge, isn't enough to protect the financial system from large losses.

Equity capital is expensive. So, increasing the level of capital in banks, whether through a high systemic risk capital charge or in other ways will prove costly for banks. An alternative would be to create capital buffers that are less costly. One instrument proposed is Contingent Convertibles (CoCos). These are debt instruments that would convert into equity if a bank's equity falls below a desired level.

One problem with the proposal is that CoCos, while cheaper than equity, would certainly be more expensive than subordinated debt. They would thus raise the cost of capital of a bank. Another problem is whether it is possible for investors to arrive at a reasonable estimate of the probability of a bank's equity capital falling below the minimum, that is, whether they can judge the risks of a bank accurately enough. Without such an estimate, it is difficult to price the instrument correctly. We know how difficult it is even for regulators to assess the riskiness of bank with all the information they have.

Another proposal is to have SIFIs buy insurance (from unlevered institutions, foreigners, or governments) that would infuse capital into these banks when capital drops below the required level.[17] Here again, the issue is the ability of investors to be able to assess risks in banks and price insurance properly.

Mechanisms for Orderly Resolution
in the Event of Failure

Large banks are routinely bailed out using taxpayer money because we do not have orderly mechanisms for resolving such banks when they fail. Such mechanisms would let equity and debt holders (and, perhaps, depositors with deposits above the guarantee limit) bear the losses while activities that are judged to be crucial to the economy (such as payments) are kept running.

We have not had orderly mechanisms for resolution in the past. That is why governments rush to bail out large banks using tax payer money. Following the financial crisis, there is an effort to end this state of affairs by putting the onus for resolution on large financial institutions themselves.

They have been asked to provide regulators with "living wills" that spell out how resolution can take place in the event of failure. These living wills would necessarily include details of loss absorbing capacity (LAC) at these banks. The Dodd-Frank Act in the United States has provisions for living wills for SIFIs and it also creates a new resolution authority called the Orderly Liquidation Authority (OLA), which grants the Federal Deposit Insurance Corporation (FDIC) the authority for resolving large financial institutions of the sort it enjoys in the case of insured depository institutions.

Banks first submitted living wills in 2012. In 2014, the FDIC told 11 Wall Street banks that their plans were not credible. Banks resubmitted living wills. In April 2016, five of the eight banks that had made submissions were told that their livings wills were found to be not credible by both the Fed and the FDIC. The living wills of two banks were each found credible by one out of the two regulators. Only one bank, Citigroup, passed the test.

There is profound skepticism about whether living wills will ever work in practice.[18] First, we are talking of banks that are large, complex, and opaque. These are banks with hundreds of thousands of employees in over a 100 countries and with over 2,000 legal entities. Even insiders find it hard to judge the risks in such banks, so to expect regulators to get a fix on these and ensure that they have been provided for in living wills does appear unrealistic. Moreover, cross-border resolution of assets and liabilities poses formidable challenges. This explains why the living wills proposed thus far have been rejected by the regulators.

If this is the case with banks, what about nonbanks? We know that it was nonbanks such as Bear Stearns and Lehman Brothers that precipitated the financial crisis. And yet no nonbank has thus far been designated as systemically important and hence subject to the prudential requirements that large banks have been subjected to. Can the markets be persuaded that these can be resolved in an orderly fashion?

Second, there are serious question marks about making loss-absorbing capacity (LAC) the key to resolution. This implies that as long as banks will ensure that there is sufficient LAC, resolution will not be a problem.

LAC consists of equity and debt that converts into equity (the CoCos we mentioned earlier are an example of such debt). The idea in having a debt portion that converts into equity is that such debt will be cheaper than equity itself. But if investors believe that there is a high likelihood of the debt getting converted into equity, they are bound to price it closer to equity. In such cases, convertible debt will be cheaper only if investors misprice risk but, then, such an instrument is unlikely to be successful over the long run—investors will have little appetite for an instrument that does not price in risk accurately.[19]

Third, the banking world is unwilling to accept the level of LAC that would be meaningful. Total LAC at some of the biggest banks in the United States is about 4–5 percent of total assets whereas a realistic estimate of the amount of LAC to make banks safe, we have seen in Chapter 3, would be 20 to 30 percent. Banks oppose such levels of LAC, saying that they would be too costly for the economy.

Last, it's not clear who would hold the bail-in debt and who would insure them through derivatives. If large financial institutions hold it, then a fall in value of the debt could lead to a systemic crisis. Ditto with large financial institutions that choose to insure such debt.

The idea of living wills for large banks is attractive in principle. When we get down to the details, however, we find that getting banks to come up with wills that would stand the test of a crisis is not simple at all.

Limiting the Scope of Banks

Another way to attack the problem of size is to reduce the scope of banks and the range of activities they are engaged in. Reducing the scope not only reduces size and complexity, it is also intended to keep banks from getting into activities that are perceived to be highly risky.

The basic idea is that banks should be using customers' deposits to engage only in core banking operations, such as making loans. They should not be getting into market-based activities that expose deposits to a high level risk—or what is often termed "casino banking."

Three broad approaches have emerged on tackling the scope of banks' activities:

a. The Volcker Rule in the United States
b. The Vickers Commission recommendations in the United Kingdom
c. The Liikanen Commission report in the European Union

The Volcker Rule

The Volcker Rule, which is part of the Dodd-Frank Act, aims at separating commercial banking activities from some investment banking activities. The Rule came into effect in the United States in July, 2015.

There are a number of reasons why such a separation is considered desirable:[20]

- There is a conflict of interest involved when a bank combines lending to a firm with securities underwriting and market-making with proprietary trading (that is, investing in securities on its own account). If the firm is not doing well, the bank may help it raise funds from the market in order to retire the loan due to the bank, a clear conflict of interest.
- Activities such as proprietary trading and hedge funds are inherently risky and can place deposits at risk. Deposits, which are covered by the government's security net, should not be used for indulging in such risky activities.
- As we saw in Chapter 2, under the earlier Basel norms, banks required less capital if they converted mortgage loans into securities and held them in the trading book. This tended to

reduce capital in the banking system and made the system more vulnerable to shocks.

- Standards of disclosure for the trading book have not been as good as those for the banking book.

These are theoretical reasons why trading by banks can lead to increase in vulnerability. In practice, does trading lead to increased vulnerability? One study attempted to answer this question.[21] It did so by trying to ascertain whether banks with a higher share of trading income before the crisis were indeed the ones that got distressed and needed official support. The sample of banks comprised 79 SIFIs across the United States, Europe, and Asia.

The findings were mixed. In the United States and Europe, a significant majority of the institutions was those with trading income to total income ratios at the extreme end of the distribution. However, similar results were not observed for Asian institutions.

When we look at anecdotal evidence, we must wonder whether investment banking by itself leads to increased vulnerability. In the financial crisis, some investment banks failed (e.g., Bear Stearns and Lehman Brothers), so did some commercial banks (Washington Mutual in the United States and Northern Rock in the United Kingdom). Some firms that combined banking and investment banking failed or ran into trouble (RBS in the United Kingdom and Citigroup in the United States). Others, such as JP Morgan Chase, weathered the crisis quite well. Similarly, some pure investment banks, such as Goldman Sachs and Morgan Stanley, emerged relatively unscathed.

However, these considerations have not deterred regulators from insisting on some separation between commercial and investment banking. The argument is not that investment banking is always riskier than commercial banking. It is that the government's safety net for banks must be limited to commercial banking activities, which are considered central to the real economy, and not to investment banking activities which are not considered as central.

Accordingly, the Volcker Rule prohibits deposit-taking institutions and entities that own them (such as BHCs) from engaging in proprietary trading or sponsoring a hedge fund or equity fund or having any equity or ownership interest in such funds.

Proprietary trading is defined as trading on the bank's account in respect of any security. Several exemptions have, however, been granted. For example:

- Transactions involving certain securities such as U.S. treasury debt or obligations of states or municipalities.
- Transactions that require underwriting or market-making in response to client or counterparty demand.
- Transactions that are in the nature of hedging risk on the bank's book.
- Transactions for securitization or sale of loans.

The problem posed by the Volcker Rule is how, in practice, proprietary trading is to be distinguished from the transactions that are exempted. In a given instance, how will the regulator determine whether securities being held by a bank are for proprietary trading or they have arisen out of, say, hedging or market-making activities?

It's not easy to tell the difference. Banks often do not hedge individual transactions or exposures. They use strategies for hedging at a portfolio level. The portfolio as a whole may be hedged without every exposure being hedged. In a given instance, how will the regulator judge that an unhedged exposure does not constitute proprietary trading? Similarly, market-making requires banks to hold securities on their own account. How do we judge that these securities are not meant for proprietary trading?

The U.S. Financial Stability Oversight Council (FSOC) has proposed certain metrics that will help regulators make these distinctions. By way of illustration, we could look at revenues arising from the trading book in relation to historical revenues or in relation to industry revenues. If the proportion is higher in relation to the benchmarks, we could reasonably conclude that the bank is indulging in proprietary trading.

Other metrics proposed include: value-at-risk (VaR, which is a standard measure of possible loss on a trading book), the proportion of trading days and the proportion of customer-initiated trades as a proportion of the inventory of securities. How these metrics will work out in practice remains to be seen.

The Volcker Rule has given rise to several concerns.

First, it appears to reverse what might be seen as the natural movement of commercial banks into investment banking activities. Following the deregulation of banking in the United States in the late 1970s and 1980s, margins in commercial banking were squeezed. This happened because depositors headed for financial markets in quest of better returns and borrowers did likewise in order to lower their borrowing costs. It was natural for banks to attempt to maintain their profitability by pursuing their clients with investment banking products. Volcker Rule thus attempts to reverse what the markets have accomplished over a long period of time.

Second, it undermines profitability of U.S.-based banks and BHCs and places them at a competitive disadvantage with respect to banks based abroad, which are not subject to similar restrictions.

Third, it will reduce liquidity of corporate securities in the United States and hence increase the liquidity premium and the borrowing costs of nonfinancial firms in the United States.

Fourth, it could push trading activities into shadow banking. This could lead to a buildup of systemic risk that is not monitored by the regulators and thus have the perverse effect of enhancing rather than reducing overall systemic risk.

These concerns notwithstanding, the United States is pushing ahead with the Volcker Rule.

The Vickers Commission Recommendations

The Independent Commission on Banking in the United Kingdom (headed by Sir John Vickers) went into the issue of making banking safer.[22] It concluded that a complete separation of retail and investment banking was not required. Instead, other ways could be found to confine the government safety net for banks to their principal operations—deposit-taking and making loans—and not protect the investment banking operations of banking companies.

At the same time, the retail portion could be insulated from any problems that might afflict the investment banking portion—the expression used by the Commission is "ring-fencing" of retail operations. The basic idea is that if a bank fails, it should be possible to resolve both the retail and the nonretail portions without extensive use of public funds. Moreover, the core banking functions, such as payment services, should not be disrupted when exogenous shocks occur.

There are costs and benefits to any regulation. An important merit of the Vickers' report is that it gives estimates of the separation it proposes and argues that the benefits far outweigh the costs. We shall touch upon these shortly. Before doing so, we shall outline the mechanisms for the separation of commercial and retail banking from investment banking.

There are two key ideas underlying the ring-fence: the *location* of the fence, that is, which activities are within the fence and which are outside; and the *height* of the fence, that is, what interconnections are permitted between activities within the fence and those outside it.

Location of the Fence

The Vickers Commission addresses a number of issues related to the location of the fence:

- Activities mandated within the fence: These would be activities whose continuous provision is imperative and for which customers do not have alternatives. Thus, the taking of deposits from and provision of overdrafts to individuals and SMEs would be required to be within the fence.
- Activities not permitted within the fence: These would include: any service which is not provided to customers within the EEA; any service which results in an exposure to a nonring-fenced bank or a nonbank financial organization, except those associated with the provision of payments services where the regulator has deemed this appropriate; trading book assets; any service which would result in a requirement to hold regulatory capital against market risk; the purchase or origination of derivatives or other contracts which would result in a requirement to hold regulatory capital against counterparty credit risk; and the purchase of loans or securities.
- Which activities should be permitted within the fence: Other banking services, such as taking deposits from customers other than individuals and SMEs and making loans to large

companies outside the financial sector should be permitted, subject to restrictions on wholesale funding of retail operations.

- Activities necessary to support certain services: There are several activities that a ring-fenced entity would need to perform in order to support certain services. For instance, it would have to protect its balance sheet against a variety of risks. Say, it would need to hedge its interest rate risk even if it could not offer this as a service to others. This may require it to buy from nonring-fenced entities derivative products. A ring-fenced entity may also need to raise wholesale funds but this would be subject to certain limits.

Thus, ring-fencing allows the majority of retail and commercial banking activities to be housed within the fence while a wholesale and investment banking is outside the fence. The Volcker Rule only prohibits certain types of investment banking activities, in particular, proprietary trading. The Vickers Commission, in contrast, asks that all investment banking activities be parked outside the fence.

There are several reasons the Commission puts forward to justify this. First, given their complexity, investment banking activities make it much more difficult to resolve a bank. Second, any activity that gives rise to market risk increases connectedness of the retail operations with financial markets and is not desirable. Third, there are several successful banks that carry out their role of intermediation without being involved in wholesale or investment banking. Fourth, removing the complexity that goes with investment banking makes it easier for the ring-fenced entity to be supervised, monitored, and managed.

Height of the Fence

The height of the fence has to do with protecting the ring-fenced entity from the risk of contagion from entities outside the fence. The key questions are whether ring-fenced entities should be part of the same corporate group that carries on activities that are prohibited within the fence; if yes, what should be the legal and economic links between the ring-fenced entity and the rest of the corporate group?

A case has been made that full separation is best for minimizing contagion. One argument is that if the ring-fenced entity is part of a larger group, it could suffer from reputational effects if any other part of the group gets into trouble. Another is that it is difficult to restrict economic links between banks within the same corporate group—firms will always find a way around the restrictions.

The Vickers Commission, however, argued that full separation is not necessary and that it is possible to limit contagion if two conditions are met:

- The retail bank is not dependent for its solvency, liquidity, or continued operations on a wider corporate group.
- The board of the retail bank is independent of the wider corporate group.

In order to ensure that these conditions are met, the Commission proposes the following measures:

- The ring-fenced entity should be created as a separate legal entity. The Commission argues that, without this, it would be difficult to monitor and impose constraints on the ring-fenced entity and its economic links with other activities.
- The entity should also be operationally separable from other activities. Only then can it continue to provide services irrespective of the health of the rest of the group and separate resolution of the ring-fenced entity and other entities in the group would be possible.
- For regulatory purposes, relationships with any entities within the same group which are not ring-fenced should not more favorably than third Party relationships. This means that all transactions with other parts of the group should be conducted on a commercial and arm's length basis in line with sound risk management practices.

One other crucial measure proposed by the Commission relates to loss-absorbing capacity. Typically, the capital that is available for absorbing losses is equity. The Commission, however, is clear that loss-absorbing capacity should include loss-absorbing debt as well or what are known as "bail-in bonds." (We referred to these previously.)

The Commission notes that loss-absorbing capacity of 16 to 24 percent of risk-weighted assets would have sufficed to absorb the losses of 95 percent of banks in a range of financial crises.[23] The midpoint of this range is 20 percent of risk-weighted assets. The Commission feels that midpoint is a desirable target for loss-absorbing capacity to aim for.

What would loss-absorbing capacity consist of? The Commission proposes the following:

- Equity capital (Tier 1) of 7 percent of risk-weighted assets (RWA) as per Basel III norms
- The higher countercyclical buffer of 2.5 percent of RWA proposed under Basel III or a ring-fence buffer of 3 percent depending on the size of the bank (the latter if the RWA to GDP of the bank is more than 3 percent)
- Nonequity (Tier 2) capital of 3.5 percent as per Basel III norms
- Bail-in bonds of 3.5 percent of RWA
- In addition to the preceding, regulators should be able to impose an additional 3 percent of capital on banks that are difficult to resolve

Adding up the aforementioned, we get a requirement of capital in the range of 17–20 percent, which the Commission feels would be adequate to cover the range of losses incurred in typical financial crises. The Commission also proposes minimum leverage ratios for banks, again depending on their size.

The capital and leverage requirements are summarized in Table 4.3.

We turn now to the costs and benefits of the proposed separation. The Commission identifies the costs as follows:

- Higher funding costs resulting from higher regulatory capital and loss absorbency.
- Requirements and also from the markets' perception of reduced diversification.

Table 4.3 Prudential capital constraints applying to ring-fenced banks

Size	Equity	Leverage ratio	Primary loss absorbing capacity	Comments
All ring-fenced banks		Tier 1>3 percent		In a resolution, insured depositors rank ahead of all unsecured creditors
RWA between 1 and 3 percent of UK GDP	Sliding scale for minimum equity-to-RWA of between 7 and 10 percent	Sliding scale for minimum leverage ratio of between 3 and 4.06 percent	Sliding scale for minimum capital +bail-in bonds of between 10.5 and 17 percent of RWA	Supervisor has discretion to increase primary loss absorbing capacity by up to 3 percentage points
RWA of more than 3 percent of UK GDP	Minimum equity-to-RWA of 10 percent	Minimum leverage ratio of 4.06 percent	Capital and bail-in-bonds should be at least 17 percent of RWA	Supervisor has discretion to increase primary loss absorbing capacity by up to 3 percentage points

Source: Julian TS Chow and Jay Surti, Making Banks Safer: Can Volcker and Vickers Do It? *IMF Working Paper*, November 2011.

- Thanks to the restrictions on the ability to transfer funds, the market would require the ring-fenced or the nonring-fenced entity to improve its capital and liquidity position and this too would mean higher cost of funding.
- Higher costs arising from the curtailment of the implicit government guarantee to the portion outside the ring fence.
- Operational costs of creating separate subsidiaries for various operations.

The Commission estimates the annual pretax cost to UK banks of the above at £4–7 billion, with the implicit government guarantee accounting for half of this cost. The social costs would be lower for two reasons: The removal of the government guarantee is not a social cost but a benefit; second, some of the private costs arise from the debt level going down in banks and hence the tax benefit going down, which again are not social costs. After making adjustments for the previous two factors, the Commission reckons that the social cost would be in the range of £1–3 billion or 0.1–0.2 percent of UK GDP.

The benefit of the package is that the banking system becomes more stable, that is, the probability of a financial crisis reduces. The annual cost of a financial crisis is estimated at 3 percent of GDP or £40 billion for the United Kingdom. Thus, the reform package would be a success even if reduced the probability of a crisis by between one-fortieth and one-thirteenth.

An alternative approach would be to estimate the impact of the higher costs of banks on the lending rate and hence on GDP. The Commission estimates that the £4–7 billion private cost of UK banks would amount to a decline in GDP of £1 billion, compared to the cost of a financial crisis of £40 billion.

Thus, whichever way one looks at it, it appears that benefits of ring-fencing outweigh the costs for British banks. In December 2013, the Financial Services (Banking Reform) Act, which incorporates various recommendations of the Vickers Commission, received Royal Assent. The measures will become effective from 2019. However, secondary legislation to enact the provisions of the Act will be necessary.

Liikanen Report

In October, 2012, a group headed by Erik Liikanen, Governor of the Central Bank of Finland, submitted a report on reform of banking in the European Union. The principal recommendations of the report were:[24]

- Proprietary trading should be hived off as a separate activity if a bank's trading assets exceed €100 billion or 15 to 25 percent of total assets. Trading can be part of the same group but it should be supported by its own capital. The bank is, however, allowed to provide hedging services to clients.
- If resolution of a bank is considered difficult, regulators should attempt to separate out other investment banking activities as well from the bank.
- A bank should have bail-in debt as one of the elements of loss-absorbing capital.
- The report has asked for more robust risk weights in determining minimum capital standards. It also urges greater prudence in real estate lending including prescription of maximum loan-to-value ratios.
- Finally, the group asks for strengthening of existing corporate governance reforms through measures such as strengthening boards and management, promoting the risk management, function, reining in compensation for bank management and staff, improving risk disclosure, and strengthening sanctioning powers.

In January 2014, the European Commission proposed legislation that departed from the Liikanen report in two key respects. One, it contains a Volcker-style prohibition and, second, it does not make separation of commercial and investment banking activities mandatory. The Volcker-style prohibition is proposed to kick off from January 1, 2017 and the Vickers-style separation from July 1, 2018.

The Volcker-style prohibition will apply to:

(i) EU global-SIFIs (and all their branches and subsidiaries regardless of their location); and

(ii) Banks that for 3 years have total assets of at least 30 billion euro
     and trading assets of 70 billion euro or 10 percent of total assets.

The prohibition applies to proprietary trading, investments in AIFs
save for closed-ended and unleveraged AIFs and investments in other
entities which themselves engage in proprietary trading or investment in
AIFs.

The Vickers-style separation of trading activities from retail and commercial banking is not mandatory. Regulators are free to judge whether,
in a given case, separation is required depending on the risk posed by
each individual core credit institution. Where risk levels are exceeded (in
relation to certain metrics that will be specified) and there is a threat to
financial stability arising from a given financial institution, the regulator
can ask for separation and ring-fencing.

Will Restrictions on Scope Help?

As we said earlier, the benefits of separating investment banking from
commercial banking activities are clear enough. Separation limits con-
tamination disruption from riskier investment banking activities. When
there are problems on the investment banking side, depositors do not
have fear the fall-out. The real economy can continue to get the benefit
of loans.

Disruption from investment banking activities was all too evident
during the financial crisis of 2007. Losses on the trading bank eroded
bank capital and led to a serious crisis of confidence among depositors.
To contain the fall-out, the scope of deposit insurance was extended considerably. In some economies, the guarantees became unlimited. Avoiding
these disruptions may be called the "crisis-time benefit" of separation.[25]

Without separation, investment banking activities get the benefit of cheaper funds. Within an organization that combines the two,
investment banking tends to appropriate superior human and financial
resources. This was reflected in the way trading books increased in size
six times that of the banking book in the United Kingdom in the period
2000 to 2007. Investment banking salaries rose four times as much as
commercial banking salaries in the period 1980 to 2007. These outcomes may lead to superior private benefit but they are not optimal from

society's point of view. Preventing such an outcome is the "normal times" benefit of separation.[26]

The practical question is whether the Volcker, Vickers, and Liikanen measures will achieve the intended objectives. All aim at legal, financial, and operational separation of activities. However, all have loopholes of some degree.

The Volcker Rule only asks for proprietary trading to be separated. The Vickers Commission mandates only deposit-taking and overdrafts to be within the ring-fence. Liikanen is judged to allow several derivative activities to be conducted within the ring-fence.

The cultures of commercial and investment banking are very different. Whether these differences can be maintained—and the mixing of human and financial resources prevented—when both are housed within the same roof (namely, one corporate group) remains a big question.

Limiting the Size of Banks

A more direct approach to the TBTF problem would be to simply limit the size of banks. As the argument goes: If a bank is too big to fail, it is too big to exist in the first place.

Simon Johnson, a professor at MIT, has been virtually leading a crusade to limit the size of banks. The case for limiting the size of banks is best made by summarizing his views on the subject. Johnson thinks that banks' size should be capped at 2 percent of GDP. Banks larger than that would face significantly higher capital charges that would serve as in incentive for their shareholders and boards to break them up into smaller banks.[27]

Size is to be measured by the total exposure of BHCs, including on-balance sheet assets, off-balance sheet items and derivatives for all subsidiaries. At the end of 2014, U.S. GDP was $17.7 trillion. Applying the cap proposed by Johnson, no bank can have an exposure of over $350 billion. This would impact 10 U.S. banks whose exposure exceeds this limit.

Johnson concedes that measures have been taken since the financial crisis to increase capital requirements for banks, improve their resolution, and limit risk-taking activities. However, these measures, he feels, may not be adequate to prevent damage to the economy arising from the failure of a large financial firm.

He points out that the increase in capital since 2008 has been modest—instead of being funded 96–97 percent by debt, banks are now funded 95 percent by debt. While resolution regimes have been improved, there is still uncertainty over how global losses would be allocated and which creditors would receive protection in the event of failure. The effectiveness of the Volcker Rule and other measures in containing risk is yet to be tested.

Johnson thinks that a limit on bank size would be more effective. "A size cap would therefore serve as a form of failsafe—if other dimensions of regulation prove insufficient, at least we can limit the maximum damage from the failure of a large financial firm."

Here, one might add a couple of other reasons for not having large banks that are frequently mentioned in the debate on big banks. One, the bigger the banks, the greater their power to influence regulations through lobbying. Such lobbying and lax regulation are believed to be among the reasons for the financial crisis of 2007.

Second, when big banks are found to have violated laws and regulations, the authorities are reluctant to initiate criminal proceedings against top management for fear of the uncertainty or turmoil this would create in the banking sector—this is simply a case of "too big to jail."

Mervyn King, former Governor of the Bank of England, sums up the situation as "too big to fail, too big to sail and too big to jail."[28] Big banks cannot be allowed to fail, they are too big to manage and those at the top at these banks do not face jail sentences for serious failures or offences.

Johnson says that the Dodd-Frank Act empowers the Fed and the FDIC to determine whether banks have a sufficiently convincing plan for bankruptcy. The plan must demonstrate that there are no systemic consequences arising from bankruptcy. If it does not, then the authorities have the right to impose appropriate requirements, including additional capital requirement. Johnson contends that it would be entirely reasonable for the Fed and the FDIC to impose additional capital requirements of an order that make it worthwhile for the bank's boards and shareholders to break up the bank.

Johnson addresses a number of concerns about limiting bank size. Would it impact U.S. economic growth adversely? He thinks not, because until the mid-1990s banks in the United States were much smaller. There is nothing to suggest that as they grew bigger, the U.S. economy bene-fited. On the contrary, they did contribute to the banks' ability to take bigger risks, which led up to the financial crisis.

Nor is it true that limits on size in the United States would disadvan-tage U.S. banks vis-à-vis their competitors in Europe—America's banks are bigger. China may have some banks that are bigger but the Chinese banking system, Johnson argues, is hardly a model for the United States.

Johnson also makes the point that his idea is not as radical as it sounds. The United States has had legislation since 1994 that kept any bank from having more than 10 percent of retail deposits. American banks got round this restriction through resort to wholesale funding. Moreover, the Dodd-Frank Act sets concentration limits that prevent any financial firm from having more than 10 percent of the aggregate liabilities of all financial firms. This limit, however, does not relate bank size to GDP, which may be more crucial to containing systemic risk.

Ross Levine of the University of California raises serious questions about the TBTF problem and the means proposed to address it.[29] Assum-ing, he says, that Dodd-Frank Act and Basel norms do not address the issue of systemic risk, he asks whether breaking up big banks is the answer.

Levine asks what the basic issue with TBTF is. It's not tax payers' losses, he argues. In the recent financial crisis, banks repaid the tax payer money infused into them with interest. He also contends that the crisis and its long-lasting repercussions had little to do with tax payers' losses.

The basic problem with TBTF, he says, is that it distorts incentives for risk-taking. Because they are not monitored properly creditors, bankers will take excessive risks. This will "lead to an inefficient allocation of society's sav-ings, reduce the quality of banking services, and hurt economic prosperity."

Would the break-up of big banks resolve the issues of monitoring and incentives? It would if it led to better monitoring, improved governance and incentives in banks. Can we expect to see these happen?

No, says Levine. There could a large number of small banks whose assets are highly correlated (as happened in the Saving and Loan crisis in the United States in the 1990s). There could be small banks that are highly interconnected so that they cannot be allowed to fail. In these cir-cumstances, debt holders would be confident of a bailout, so would lack the incentives for closer monitoring.

Even if monitoring by debt holders improves, banks might find ways to raise funds that circumvent larger debtors who are the ones capable of monitoring banks closely. Monitoring by equity holders is quite poor, so monitoring by debt holders alone may not improve governance. If the problem is primarily one of incentives for managers, this problem should be addressed in ways that are more effective than simply breaking up large banks.

There are a few other concerns one might add:

- How exactly do we go about breaking up large banks so that they meet the cap on size of two percent of GDP? Do we ask them to shed particular businesses? Or do we expect them to sell portions of various businesses, in other words, they scale down various businesses?
- Do we have buyers for the large amounts of businesses that will be on sale? Do these buyers have the expertise to run the businesses?
- In economies that are smaller than the United States, a cap of 2 percent of GDP would render limit the ability of domestic banks to compete with larger global banks. If, however, we had a higher cap on size, that may defeat the purpose of containing systemic risk.

Thus, even if we accept that the idea of limiting the size of banks is good in principle, we are faced with questions about how we attain this idea in practice.

Conclusion

The reforms we covered in Chapter 3 do not address a fundamental issue in financial crises: the TBTF. Banks have been growing bigger and bigger in order to reap the benefits of economies of scale and scope. However, it's not clear that, beyond a certain asset size, increase in size results in lower unit costs.

Even if such benefits do exist, they must be weighed against the systemic risk posed by large banks. When banks grow very large, it tends to distort incentives for bankers. They can take huge risks in the confidence that the banks will not be allowed to fail.

Various reforms have been proposed for the TBTF problem. One, an increase in capital requirements that is intended to disincentivize banks from growing too big. Two, limits on the scope of operations of banks. Three, limits on the absolute size of banks. Four, living wills that will ensure orderly resolution of large banks in a crisis.

The first two have been implemented in some advanced economies. The third has thus far remained in the area of discourse. The fourth is still work in progress. We lack the confidence today that we have cracked the TBTF problem.

CHAPTER 5

A Safer World of Banking: Out of the Box Proposals

We have seen in Chapters 3 and 4 that regulators have been hard at work trying to fix problems in the world of banking. Nearly a decade after the financial crisis, it's worth asking: Are we confident that banking is safer today as a result? Is the probability of a crisis considerably lower than a decade ago? And do the proposals we have discussed thus far in this book go far enough in ensuring financial stability?

There are some measures on which the banking system certainly appears stronger today than during the financial crisis:

- In the United States, the top five banks had a common equity Tier 1 ratio which was higher than that specified by Basel III; all but one bank even surpassed the higher requirements imposed by the U.S. Fed.[1]
- In the Euro area, significant institutions saw the same ratio rise from 9 percent in 2012 to 13 percent by early 2016.[2]
- In June 2016, all but 2 of the top 33 banks in the United States passed the Fed's "stress tests" that evaluate how such firms would fare in a financial crisis. This showed that banks have enough capital to weather a financial crisis and it appeared to suggest that the attempt to shore up capital at banks was bearing fruit.[3] In the same months, most of the 51 banks surveyed in the Euro area likewise passed "stress tests."[4]
- The loan-to-deposit ratio is an indicator of safety in banking. Loans are illiquid. So, the lower the ratio, the more liquid a bank is. If there is a demand for deposits, banks can sell securities to

Table 5.1 Loan-to-deposit ratio at U.S. banks

2007	90.7%
2008	84.6%
2009	78.0%
2010	77.5%
2011	72.6%
2012	70.4%
2013	69.7%
2014	69.8%
2015	72.0%

Source: FDIC.

meet the demand for deposits. In the United States, the ratio has fallen from 91 percent in 2007 to 72 percent in 2015, as Table 5.1 shows. This points to increased stability. The ratio of deposits to liabilities is also a measure of stability. The higher the deposits, the lesser the dependence on short-term borrowings. In the United States, the ratio of deposits to liabilities has risen from 73 percent in 2007 to 86 percent in 2015.

As against these positive factors, we have concerns that we outlined in Chapter 4. Banks are bigger, more complex, and still highly interconnected. They are still too-big-to-fail (TBTF) and hence the risk-taking incentives for managers that go with TBTF are very much there.

Not least, concentration in the banking sector (defined as the share of the top three banks in total banking assets) has increased when we would have liked it to go down (Table 5.3). The greater the concentration, the more vulnerable the banking sector is: The failure of a few banks can impact hugely the sector as a whole.

Several economists and banking professionals are of the view that the changes in regulation of the sort we have seen since the crisis are not enough to avert another major financial crisis. They believe that radical changes in policy are required. We need to think out of the box if we are to prevent recurrent financial crises that devastate economies.

In what follows, we examine some proposals that have been put forward and make one proposal of our own.

Table 5.2 Deposit or total liabilities in U.S. banks

2007	72.9%
2008	72.5%
2009	79.3%
2010	79.6%
2011	82.5%
2012	84.2%
2013	85.5%
2014	85.1%
2015	85.9%

Source: FDIC.

Table 5.3 Bank concentration ratio in select advanced economies

Country	2007	2014
France	62.34	68.27
Germany	73.63	98.60
United States	33.95	35.75
United Kingdom	59.36	72.11

Source: Global Financial Development Database, World Bank.

Mian and Sufi

The description of the crisis of 2007 as a "financial crisis" assumes that banks were at the heart of the problem of the recession that followed. In Chapter 1, we pointed out that this view has been challenged by some, notably by the economists Atif Mian and Amir Sufi.[5] They argue that the problem was one of household debt going up to unsustainable levels, that is, levels that could not be sustained by the incomes of the households concerned.

Many borrowed large amounts from banks in order to invest in housing without regard for their ability to pay. They hoped that housing prices would keep rising and that they could borrow against the increase in prices to refinance at lower rates the loans they had taken for the purchase of their homes. When housing prices fell, they found themselves unable to do so. The borrowers were stuck with loans they could not repay or found difficult to repay.

In this situation, borrowers can default. Lenders will then foreclose the property and try to find a buyer. This causes housing prices to fall further and imposes losses on lenders. Alternatively, borrowers can continue to pay their loans by cutting back on spending on other things—this causes demand in the economy to fall and unemployment to rise. A third course is for borrowers to sell their houses at values less than the value of the loans they owe. In that case, borrowers will have to use some of their own savings to repay loans. This again results in a loss of wealth to borrowers and cutbacks in spending.[6]

Whatever the course of action borrowers opt for, the economy suffers. Mian and Sufi argue that the way to contain the adverse impact on the economy would have been for lenders to forgive some of the debts owed by borrowers. This would have meant that lenders and borrowers would have shared the losses arising from the fall in housing prices. Lenders (or the investors in banks) are typically people who are better off than borrowers. The marginal propensity to consume of wealthier people is less than that of people who are not wealthy. As a result, had losses been shared by lenders and borrowers, the fall in consumption—and the impact of the economy—would have been less severe than when borrowers had to bear all the losses.[7]

Unfortunately, debt forgiveness was rendered difficult for various reasons. Household mortgages had been securitized and a servicer represented the holders of mortgage-backed securities (MBS). There was no bank that borrowers could turn to for renegotiation. That apart, there was a general reluctance to write off debt for fear of moral hazard.

There was an apprehension that even those who could service their loans might start asking for renegotiation of their debts. There was also the fear that writing off debts would set a bad precedent for the future: Borrowers would try not to pay back their loans hoping to get some of it written off. Thus, the problem of high household debt remained addressed, banks suffered huge losses, consumption fell sharply and the recession stretched out for long.[8]

The central problem, Mian and Sufi contend, is not the banking system but high levels of debt and the difficulty in renegotiating debt contracts when borrowers have genuine problems in servicing their debts. The issue we need to address, therefore, is the inflexibility of debt contracts.

For instance, when a student takes a loan to finance his graduate education, he has no means of knowing what the jobs market will be like when he graduates. If jobs become difficult to find when he graduates, it would not be correct to expect him to service the debt in full. In other words, some financial contracts must be designed so that the lender shares the downside risk and also the upside risk. We need contracts that look less like debt and more like equity.

Mian and Sufi propose "shared-responsibility mortgages" (SRMs) as a way of preventing financial crises.[9] Such mortgages would have two characteristics: (i) the lender offers downside protection the borrower; and (ii) the borrower gives up 5 percent capital gain to the lender on the upside.

In a standard fixed-rate mortgage, the annual payment to be made by the borrower remains the same, whether the price of the house goes up or goes down. When the home value goes down, the borrower's spending declines because of the "wealth effect" (the borrower feels poorer now). If the borrower chooses to continue to service the loan, the decline in his spending is exacerbated.

The Mian-Sufi proposal gives the borrower protection on the downside by linking mortgage payments to a local house-price index. For instance, if the house-price index is 100 at the time the loan is taken and it later falls by 30 percent after a year, the borrower's mortgage payment would also fall by 30 percent in the second year. At the same time, the amortization schedule would be the same as fixed originally, that is, the mortgage balance would go down as per the original formula. So, if the price decline of 30 percent stays for the remaining 29 years, in effect, 30 percent of the principal payment is written off.

The lender loses when the home price falls. He has to be compensated, therefore, through a share in any capital gain the borrower may realize while selling or refinancing the house. Using data on the growth and volatility in housing prices, Mian and Sufi estimate that a 5-percent share of the capital gain adequately compensates the lender for the downside protection given to the borrower.

The advantage of SRM is that when housing prices decline, the borrower retains the same percentage of home equity as before even though the value of the home equity would be proportionately smaller than before.

Suppose the value of a home is $100,000 and the owner has made a down payment of $20,000 and takes a mortgage of $80,000. If the value of the house falls by 30 percent, the house is worth $70,000. This value will now belong entirely to the bank to whom the borrower owes $80,000–the home owner' own equity of $20,000 is wiped out.

In an SRM, the mortgage is also worth 30 percent less, that is, $56,000. The owner's equity in the home is thus worth $14,000 ($70,000 minus $56,000). The home owner's equity is thus worth less than before. But it's not wiped out, as would have been the case if the value of the mortgage had remained unchanged at $80,000–it remains at the original proportion of 20 percent.

Mian and Sufi quantify the benefits that SRMs would have conferred on the U.S. economy in the financial crisis. The main advantage is that they would have prevented foreclosures of homes and the consequent fall in house prices and aggregate spending. Mian and Sufi estimate that for every 1 percent of owners that went into foreclosure, house prices fell by 1.9 percent between 2007 and 2009.[10]

Since 5.1 percent of houses went into foreclosure, SRMs would have prevented a decline in house prices of 9.6 percent. This was 46 percent of the 21 percent decline in house prices in the period. Taking into account the total loss of wealth on account of the fall in housing prices, the authors estimate that SRMs would have prevented a loss of $2.5 trillion in housing wealth, which would have meant additional spending of $150 billion.

SRMs would impact the economy in another way. They involve a transfer of losses from borrowers to lenders, that is, from those with a lower marginal propensity to consume (MPC) to a higher MPC. The authors estimate the value of this transfer at $451 billion, which, in turn, would have meant higher spending by home owners of $54 billion. Thus, SRMs would have brought about an additional spending of $150 plus $54 billion or $204 billion. By way of comparison, the government fiscal stimulus in 2009 was worth $550 billion. Thus, SRMs would have provided a stimulus equivalent to half the fiscal stimulus without any increase in government debt.

Mian and Sufi argue that the reason instruments such as SRMs have not sprung up is that the government incentivizes the use of debt by the financial system in many ways—by allowing tax deductibility on interest payments, guaranteeing deposits, implicit too-big-to-fail subsidies, and so on. But the issue of debt instruments on the present scale imposes costs on tax payers through frequent financial crises.

The SRM principle may be applied to contexts other than household debt. Sovereign debt contracts could involve sharing of risk. For instance, interest payments on sovereign debt could be linked to nominal GDP. The authors do not suggest this but, perhaps, corporate debt could also include some sharing of risk.

The bottom line is clear enough: Excessive debt is the root cause of financial crises. The enduring solution thus lies not just in making the banking system more resilient but in reducing the issue of inflexible debt contracts and opting instead for instruments where risks are shared between borrower and lender.

Adair Turner

Mian and Sufi contend that debt is the problem that economies need to fix. And their way of doing so is to introduce an element of flexibility in debt contracts by incorporating some features of equity. This approach takes the creation of large amounts of debt as a given but would like to mitigate its effects.

In his book, Adair Turner outlines a more radical approach.[11] He would like to attack the problem of debt head-on by limiting the amount of debt creation itself. He examines some of the solutions proposed and why he thinks they may not work. Next, he spells out how we should address the basic drivers of credit growth in the modern economy. Finally, he outlines a scheme for managing the quantity and mix of debt that is created.

Solutions Proposed

In the fractional reserve system we have, banks have the ability to create credit. For every $100 of deposit, banks need to keep only a small fraction as reserves with the central bank. The rest can be given as loans. Out of the loans given, again only a fraction needs to be kept as reserves, the rest can give rise to more loans. This is what is known as the "banking multiplier"—one dollar of deposit can translate into, say, five dollar of credit.

We can curb excess credit by curbing credit itself. This can be done by abolishing fractional banking. Banks can be asked to park all 100 percent of their deposits as reserves and confine themselves to putting through payments. They cannot make loans. Several leading figures of the Chicago School of Economics—Henry Simons, Irving Fisher, and Milton Friedman—have favored this approach.

Turner argues that this may not be desirable. If banks don't create credit (and money), all money creation will have to be done by the government. The government can run up expenditure that will be financed by notes printed by the central bank. Just as the private sector can create excess money, so can the government. And we can't be sure that the government will spend the money efficiently. Leaving money creation entirely to government is as bad as leaving it entirely or mostly to the private sector.[12]

A second approach is to remove tax incentives for debt and, indeed, to tax transactions that involve transforming short-term liabilities into long-term assets. This would raise the price of credit and thus reduce credit creation. While these measures have been advocated for long, however, policy makers lack the appetite for them.

Any radical change in taxation of debt would lead to windfall gains and losses and there would be political opposition. We do not have global coordination of tax policy. If some governments choose not to tax debt, then cross-border lending could reduce the effectiveness of any attempt government's attempt to tax debt. We are still far off from any reform in the way debt is treated.

Then we have Mian-Sufi's suggestion to introduce SRMs. The problem that Turner sees in SRMs is that borrowers have to share some of the upside and they may be averse to the idea. Second, SRMs could give rise to a class of securities that are linked to housing prices. As people begin to bet on housing prices, volatility would increase. Thus, the objective of protecting borrowers against price risk gets defeated.

The proposed solutions thus all have significant shortcomings. We need to find other ways to curb excessive creation of credit.

Curbing Drivers of Credit

Turner says that there are three main drivers of credit growth today: real estate, rising inequality, and global imbalances.[13] Each must be tackled if we are to prevent excessive creation of credit.

Real estate is a source of instability for several reasons. Real estate prices keep rising as the supply of land is limited but the demand for land keeps rising as income grows. The world is now increasingly driven by information technology. As the prices of capital goods that incorporate information technology fall, the share of real estate in capital investment is bound to rise. By far the biggest chunk of all lending in the advanced economies (60 percent) is accounted for by real estate.

Housing accounts for a significant portion of all wealth in modern societies. Hence rising land prices account for the large rise in the wealth to income ratio in advanced economies in the past 40 years. When the wealth-to-income ratio is high, a small change in wealth—caused by fluctuation in asset prices, such as the price of land—can cause a large change in income. This significantly impacts consumption and investment.

Public policy must, therefore, address increases in real estate prices. One way would be to regulate lending to real estate through higher loan-to-value ratios and higher capital requirements for real estate lending. Tax policies must also remove or reduce incentives for investment in housing. Urban development must be planned so as to avoid concentration of the population in a few places, a factor that causes real estate prices to rise.

Inequality has its own implications for credit growth. As a small section of the population garners more and more of the national income, aggregate demand rises less rapidly than if the income were spread out more equitably. This is because the marginal propensity to consume of the rich is less than that of those in lower income groups. Under such circumstances, we need credit growth to fuel growth in aggregate demand. An unequal society, Turner says, is also a "credit-intensive" economy and a potentially unstable one.

The problem of excess credit thus requires us to address the issue of inequality. This requires action of several fronts: investing in skills and education; tax policies; labor market intervention (such as basic minimum wage for all).

Lastly, Turner sees global imbalances as a driver of growth. This follows from the argument we touched upon in Chapter 2. The argument is that current account deficits in some countries are financed by capital flows from countries with current account surpluses. Excess deficits mean excess capital flows that drive down interest rates in countries receiving such inflows and boost credit.

Managing the Quantity and Mix of Debt

Credit booms are often a precursor to crises. Excess credit leads to cutbacks in consumption and investment that drag down economic growth. How do we contain credit booms? The standard prescription is to raise interest rates. The economist Knut Wicksell argued that interest rates must be kept in alignment with the "natural interest rate" which was the return on real projects.

By way of illustration, suppose the global economy is growing at 5 percent, interest rates should be kept at about that level. Prior to 2008, money interest rates were below that level, and this created incentives for borrowing.

However, there is a problem with using interest rates to dampen credit booms. Different sectors will respond differently to an interest rate increase depending on the return in a given sector compared with the interest rate. There is no single natural rate of interest for all sectors but different rates for different sectors depending on the marginal productivity of new investment. Thus, the interest rate may not be effective enough in containing credit booms.[14]

We have mentioned some other means of constraining credit growth: higher capital requirements for banks and countercyclical capital requirements. Turner also considers higher reserve ratios for banks, that is, the proportion of liabilities that banks keep as cash with central banks. Keeping higher reserves with central banks limits the funds available with banks themselves and so raises the cost of funds or the interest rate. The shortcomings in the use of interest rates thus also apply to the use of higher reserves.

Turner argues that the risk-weights that banks are required to use for various types of lending may capture potential losses to banks. But they do not capture the costs to the economy of excess lending to sectors such as real estate. He argues that risk weights must be designed in ways that reflect the social costs of certain types of lending, especially lending to real estate.

Turner supports the measures to ensure that credit growth we have mentioned earlier: stipulating loan to value ratios and ring-fencing of core banking activities. We also need credit to go to the right sectors for investment purposes and we must ensure it is not skewed toward real estate. Specialized financial institutions for power, renewable energy, SMEs need to be encouraged so that there is adequate credit flow to these sectors—many economies do have such institutions.

Turner's reform agenda is thus premised on the belief that credit creation and allocation cannot be entirely left to free markets. Government intervention is required to ensure that credit allocation happens in ways that are socially desirable. The proposal smacks of centralized planning and could mean that less credit is available than before in the advanced economies. If we accept that the financial sectors in these economies have become bloated, that would not be a bad thing at all.

Mervyn King

We referred previously to the idea of "fractional" banking, that is, banks parking some portion of their deposits as reserves with the central bank. We also mentioned the proposal to abolish such banking and to have 100 percent of deposits parked as reserves.

In such a case, how would banks make loans? Well, they could make loans by raising debt and equity for the purpose. So we would have a "narrow" bank that carries out payment services and backed by deposits and a "wide bank" backed by debt and equity. If loans go bad, equity and debt holders will bear losses. Deposits are not affected, so the payment system is not disrupted.

Mervyn King, former governor of the Bank of England, argues that, in such a system, the link between the creation of credit and the creation of money would be broken.[15] Banks can no longer create money out of deposits by keeping only a fraction of deposits as reserves and lending the rest. A basic definition of money is that it is the sum of currency and deposits.

When all the deposits are parked as reserves with the central bank, the multiplication of deposits—and hence the creation of money—is no longer possible. Credit booms and busts would thus become a thing of the past.

Why would governments not opt for such an obvious solution? There are problems. One is that a move toward complete separation of narrow and wide banking would be disruptive for the banking system. Banks would have to raise enough debt and equity to support the loans they have. If they cannot, they will have to reduce the amount of loans they hold.

Second, financing loans entirely through debt and equity, without having a component of short-term deposits, will make loans more expensive. The transformation of short-term deposits into long-term loans does confer benefits to the economy even while it imposes risks.

Third, when we get banks to finance loans entirely through debt and equity and keep deposits out of the equation, we are not entirely eliminating disruption in the banking system or runs on banks. True, deposits remain safe and payments will not be disrupted. But, when banks finance themselves through equity and debt for the purpose of making loans, what we have is a form of collateralized borrowing—they are borrowing against loans that serve as collateral.

Any decline in the value of collateral—that is, the value of loans—means that holders of banks' debt will demand more collateral. Banks will be forced to sell some of their assets to provide collateral; this will cause asset prices to fall. Or the holders of debt will refuse to roll over their loans. Either way, we will see a contraction in credit. The contraction is less severe than in the case where deposits are used to fund loans and we have a run on deposits. But it doesn't go away. The government will still find itself obliged to provide liquidity to banks—what King calls "catastrophic insurance"—to prevent a sharp contraction in credit.[16]

Narrow banking reduces the cost of catastrophic insurance but it makes lending more expensive. Allowing the use of deposits for making loans makes loans cheaper but leads to frequent crises. Is there a way in which deposits can be used for making loans while reducing the cost of catastrophic insurance? King proposes a solution. He calls this Pawnbroker For All Seasons (PFAS). It works as follows.[17]

Central banks act as lenders of last resort (LOLR) after crisis has erupted. They have no means of knowing accurately which banks are solvent and which are not. Since banks have to be saved somehow, they also do not have the luxury of distinguishing between good and bad collateral in offering funds to banks.

King proposes that, instead, central banks decide *in advance* what sort of funds they will provide against a bank's assets. They will judge each asset of a bank and provide funds after taking a suitable "haircut," that is, withholding a fraction of the value of the asset. The "haircut" is intended to protect the central bank from any drop in the value of the asset.

Each bank would decide how much of its assets it can place in advance at the central bank for use as collateral. The central bank would decide what haircut each would take on each asset and how much cash it would be willing to lend against that asset. Adding up all the assets placed with the central bank, it would be possible to decide the total money that the bank can borrow from the central bank. This total is a measure of the liquid assets available with the bank.

On the liabilities side, the bank has demand deposits and short-term unsecured debt that could leave at short notice. The total of these two is a measure of the bank's effective liquid liabilities. King proposes that the effective liquid assets should exceed their effective liquid liabilities. In effect, banks will be required to take out liquidity insurance in normal times so that they can access central bank funds in times of crisis.

King gives a simple illustration of how his proposal would work:[18]

Consider a simple example of a bank with total assets and liabilities each equal to $100 million. Suppose that it has $10 million of assets in the form of reserves at the central bank, $40 million in holdings of relatively liquid securities and $50 million in the form of illiquid loans to businesses. If the central bank decided that the appropriate haircut on the liquid securities was 10 percent and on the illiquid loans was 50 percent, then it would be willing to lend $36 million against the former and $25 million against the latter, provided that the bank prepositioned all its assets as available collateral. The banks' effective liquid assets would be $ (10 + 36 + 25) million, a total of $71 million. It would have to finance itself with no more than $71 million of deposits and short-term debt.

King suggests that his proposal be implemented over a period of 10 to 20 years so that banks have adequate time to make adjustments to their balance sheets.

His proposal does raise issues. Since the proportion of deposits in relation to assets may have to come down in many banks, banks will have to rely more on debt and equity to finance their assets. This would raise the cost of funds for banks. Where banks cannot raise the necessary capital, they would have to sell their assets, that is, there would be contraction of credit.

Equally important, it is not easy for central banks to determine accurately the "haircut" on a wide variety of assets well in advance. Allowing them to do so confers enormous power on central banks. The higher the haircut, the greater is the funding other than deposits required to finance the asset, hence the higher the cost to the borrower. In other words, the interest rate that the borrower is charged will depend on the haircut imposed on a given asset by the central bank.

While central banks do set interest rates, they set only one reference rate. In King's scheme of things, central banks effectively assume the power to set different rates for different products, that is, they begin to determine relative prices of financial products.[19]

This amounts to centralized setting of prices that militates against the concept of a free market. It is conceptually similar to what Adair Turner has proposed, namely, setting risk weights based on the social cost of particular products. Whereas Turner would want this for a few important products such as real estate, King's proposal would result in central banks having a hand in setting prices for a wide range of assets.

The noteworthy point is that King, like Turner, believes that banks' ability to create unlimited amounts of money needs to be constrained.

A Role for Public Sector Banks

Wherever there is a market failure, there is a case for intervention through regulation. We cannot leave matters entirely to the private sector. In the case of banking, the market failures have to do with externalities.

Externalities are situations where the social cost or social benefit exceeds the private cost or private benefit. Bank failures, we have seen, have significant externalities—the broader economy tends to be affected. To prevent these failures, the government extends a safety net to banks through deposit insurance and LOLR facilities. The government is thus an implicit lender to banks. Just as any bank would lay down conditions for its borrowers, so also the government (or its arm, the central bank) lays down conditions for banks to operate.

Regulation, however, is not the only way in which government can intervene. It can also intervene through public provision of goods. That is, the government itself can run banks. This is not the norm in advanced economies except, perhaps, in Germany where public sector banks (PSBs) have a share of around 30 percent of banking assets.[20] However, in emerging markets, such as Brazil, Russia, India, and China, PSBs continue to play an important role and even a dominant one. Government ownership in Indian banking is 70 percent, in Russia 54 percent, and in Brazil 42 percent. That in China is close to 90 percent.[21]

It is noteworthy that the two fastest-growing large economies in the world, India and China, have banking systems that are dominated by PSBs. Banking systems in both the economies have not suffered a crisis in the past two decades, unlike the large number of private sector-dominated banking systems.

Is this a mere coincidence? Or can public ownership conduce to stability and efficiency in banking. In what follows, we seek to address this question by looking at the Indian experience.

Public Sector Banks: The Indian Experience

India has long had government ownership in banking. Government ownership falls into two broad phases: prereforms or the postnationalization phase (1969 to 1994) and postreform (1994 to present).

The Indian government entered the banking business by nationalizing the British-owned Imperial Bank of India in 1955. The bank came to be known thereafter as State Bank of India (SBI) and it has for long been India's biggest bank. Seven state banks became subsidiaries of SBI when they were nationalized in 1960. The next major round of nationalization happened in 1969 when 14 major banks were acquired by the government. Then, in 1980, another six banks were nationalized. In 1983, two of the nationalized banks were merged. For a long period thereafter, India had a total of 27 PSBs—SBI and its seven subsidiaries, and 19 nationalized banks.

The primary objective of bank nationalization was to increase the spread of banking or what is called "financial deepening," bringing more savings into the financial system and increasing the penetration of credit. There were other objectives as well: reducing concentration of wealth and breaking the stranglehold of private business on the banking system.

Bank nationalization made considerable progress in respect of the primary objective of the spread of banking. The Indian banking system delivered admirably on these objectives. Branches expanded from around 8,262 in 1969 to over 69,071 in 2004 giving India one of the biggest branch networks in the world. Thanks to branch expansion, there was financial deepening: the deposits to GDP ratio rose from 16.4 percent in 1971–1975 to 36.1 percent in 1989–1990. Bank credit to the commercial sector increased from 15.6 to 30.3 percent of GDP in 1989–1990.[22]

In the process, however, loan quality, efficiency, and profitability became casualties. Profit after tax of all PSBs in 1992–1993 was minus 1 percent. This does not mean that PSBs had failed. Management must be judged in relation to the performance objective. The objective given to PSBs was to grow their balance sheets. In this, they succeeded very well. However, there was clearly a need for a change of course—the course obtaining then was not sustainable.

Banking sector reforms commenced in a major way in 1993–1994, following closely on the heels of the larger economic reforms India initiated in 1991–1992. The key features of these reforms were:

- Deregulation of deposit and lending rates of banks.
- Stringent norms for income recognition, asset classification, and capital adequacy.
- Listing of PSBs on the stock market.
- Licensing of a new set of private sector banks.
- Reduction in statutory preemptions of bank liabilities for investment in government securities which freed banks to use more of their resources for lending.

In the years that have followed, these reforms have been carried forward and other reforms have been initiated. There has been a gradual liberalization of entry of foreign banks and banks specializing in particular niches (such as payments) have been permitted.

Though the public sector still dominates banking, there is today greater competition and the share of the private sector has kept growing. The share of PSBs in banking assets has declined from nearly 90 percent at the commencement of reforms to around 70 percent. Analysts expect that in about a decade from now, the share of the public sector in banking assets could fall to as much as 50 percent.

Most emerging economies opted to privatize their banking systems wholesale at some point. Typically, such privatization was a response to a banking crisis and it resulted in large foreign ownership of the banking system, as in East Asia and Eastern Europe.

India has chosen a different reform path. It has opted to retain substantial government ownership of banking while exposing PSBs to market discipline and greater competition. We will argue that this very different approach has contributed to an improvement in efficiency in the system while preserving stability consequent to reforms. We do so by examining the record on efficiency and stability, postreforms. We split the post-reform period into 1991–1992 to 2011–2012 and 2011–2012 to 2013–2014. This is because we believe that, in the latter period, the banking sector came to be impacted by several factors that were extraneous to management. Hence PSBs' performance in the latter period cannot be seen as a reflection on managerial performance.

Improvements in Efficiency

Efficiency changes can be measured on various dimensions:

i. Increase in competition

Competition has increased in Indian banking in the postreform period (Table 5.4). The share of the top five banks in assets, deposits, and profits has declined over the period, except for 2015–2016 when performance of most PSBs was adversely impacted by large nonperforming loans.

Table 5.4 Indian banking: Share of top five banks—assets, deposits, and profits (percent)

	1991–1992	1998–1999	2001–2002	2007–2008	2015–2016
	1	3	5		
Assets	51.7	44.7	43.5	38.4	39.7
Deposits	49.0	44.4	43.3	37.3	37.9
Profits	54.5	49.1	41.4	37.2	100.0

Source: Report on Trend and Progress in Banking, RBI, several issues, Indian Banks' Association (2015–2016).

Table 5.5 PSBs: Net interest margin

	1992–1995	2004–2005	2007–2008	2011–2012
	(Avg)			
All banks	2.84	2.83	2.35	2.76

Source: Report on Trend and Progress in Banking, RBI website.

ii. Net interest margin (NIM)

The NIM is the difference in the interest income and interest expense as a proportion of assets. One would expect the spread to decline consequent to deregulation. That is what deregulation is all about: It squeezes the margins of producers and leads to increase in volumes. India's banking sector has been relatively impervious to this trend. Table 5.5 shows the trend in NIM in the period since deregulation.

We see that the NIM has been surprisingly steady from 1991–1992 until 2011–2012 except for a dip in 2007–2008 (and two subsequent years which are not shown in the table). This has, of course, turned out to be a blessing for banks but it goes counter to the rationale for deregulation. It also runs counter to the experience of other banking sectors consequent to deregulation. The pressure on NIM and, hence, on profitability elsewhere is an important factor causing banking crises; the steadiness of the NIM in India is one factor underlying the absence of a similar crisis in India.

The reason that the NIM has not dropped is that disintermedia-tion—the exit of borrowers and depositors in a big way from the banking system—has not happened despite the growth of financial markets. That's because the Indian banking system started off from a low of penetration at the commencement of reforms. This meant that savers and borrowers were available to banks in large numbers over the period of deregulation.

iii. Reduction in intermediation costs

The ratio of intermediation costs to total assets has declined dramatically in the post-reform years, driven largely by the decline in the ratio in the PSB group (Table 5.6). We use 1996–1997 as the starting year in this table and the next table as accounting norms changed in the initial years of reform and hence the initial years are not comparable with the years that followed.

The most important reason is that the workforce remained constant at PSBs through the initial years in the face of rising volume of work, followed thereafter by a reduction caused by voluntary retirement schemes. It is only in the last 3 years or so that recruitment has gathered pace in PSBs. Another reason is branch rationalization. The hard work of setting up branches had been accomplished in the nationalization era, so PSBs found that they did not have to invest in branches and could, in fact, afford to close down a few.

iv. Improvement in returns

Efficiency, as measured by net profit to total assets, has shown an unambiguous improvement over the years and has touched the important figure of 1 percent in recent years. (Internationally, a 1-percent return on assets is considered a benchmark for good performance.) Even in the initial years following the subprime crisis, said to be the worst crisis in the past century, return on assets has remained over 1 percent in Indian banking (Table 5.7).

Table 5.6 PSBs: Intermediation costs to total assets ratio (percent)

	1996–1997	2004–2005	2007–2008	2011–2012
Commercial banks	2.85	2.13	1.78	1.77

Source: RBI, Report on Trend and Progress in Banking, several reports.

Table 5.7 PSBs: Net profit/ total assets (%)

	1996–1997	2004–2005	2008–2009	2009–2010	2011–2012
Commercial banks	0.67	0.89	1.0	1.05	1.08

Source: RBI, Report on Trend and Progress in Banking, several reports.

Improvement in Soundness or Financial Stability

We can judge the improvement in stability using two widely used measures: the capital adequacy ratio and the ratio of nonperforming assets (NPA) to total assets advances. As Table 5.8 shows, there has been an improvement in both these indicators.

The picture has changed since 2011–2012. Performance of PSBs has deteriorated. Return on assets has dropped to 0.54 percent (Table 5.9). One key driver of profitability, intermediation cost has changed very little over a 3-year period. Another driver, NIM, declined by 19 basis points between 2011–2012 and 2012–2013 without making any significant difference to return on assets. Between 2012–2013 and 2013–2014, there was a decline of a smaller magnitude, 12 basis points, but return on assets has fallen sharply. Clearly, the key to deterioration in profit is neither intermediation cost nor NIM.

The key is the third item in Table 5.9, namely, NPAs. Gross NPAs as a proportion of gross advances rose from 3.2 percent in 2011–2012 to 3.8 percent in 2012–2013 and further to 4.6 percent in 2013–2014.

What accounts for the increase in NPAs? As of December 2014, five sectors accounting for 25 percent of the exposure of all banks had a share of 51 percent of all stressed advances (stressed advances including NPAs as well as loans that had to be restructured and provided for as per regulatory norms). These were mining, iron and steel, infrastructure, textiles, and aviation. Of these, steel and infrastructure accounted for 40 percent of the total stressed advances. Large projects in these sectors have been impacted by certain structural failings in the economy: problems in land acquisition, delays in environmental clearances, adverse court judgments, and so on.

At PSBs, these five sectors accounted for 29 percent of the advances and 53 percent of all stressed advances. At private sector banks, they accounted for 13 percent of advances and 34 percent of stressed advances;

Table 5.8 Soundness indicators

	1996–1997	2004–2005	2006–2007	2011–2012
Net NPAs/ Advances	9.18	2.06	1.05	0.97
Capital adequacy (Basel I)	NA	12.8	12.3	13

Source: RBI, Report on Trend and Progress in Banking, RBI.

Table 5.9 Key financial ratios of PSBs in recent years

	2011–2012	2012–2013	2013–2014
Net interest margin	2.76	2.57	2.45
Intermediation cost/Total assets	1.59	1.57	1.62
Gross nonperforming loans/ Gross advances	3.2	3.8	4.6
Return on assets	0.88	0.8	0.54

Source: RBI: Statistical Tables Relating to Banks in India; Financial Stability Report.

at foreign banks, the shares were 11 and 40 percent respectively. Private and foreign banks chose to take a lower exposure to these sectors than PSBs and have been less impacted as a result. Wherever they did get exposed, they have been significantly impacted.[23]

The Indian economic boom of 2004–2008 was driven by private investment, especially investment in private infrastructure. It was PSBs that substantially funded this boom in investment and the consequent acceleration in India's growth rate to over 9 percent. They now face the downside of the loan exposures they had taken. To the extent that private banks took lower exposures, they have been less badly impacted.

In a developing economy that lacks well-developed bond markets, can we afford to have the entire banking sector shunning infrastructure and allied sectors because less risky opportunities are available aplenty in the Indian economy? Can the structural failings in the economy be taken as a reflection on the quality of management at PSBs? These points are worth keeping in mind while comparing the performance of PSBs and private sector banks in the last 2 or 3 years.

Viewed in this perspective, the deterioration in PSB performance in recent years does not take away from the trend toward improvement in performance for the greater part of the postreform period. The most striking aspect of the Indian banking system is that nearly two decades after deregulation, the system has remained free from crisis (despite the stresses of the recent years).

This is no mean achievement. Typically, deregulation sets the stage for a crisis down the road. One study estimates that the probability of a crisis rises over time following financial liberalization.[24] This is because banks find their margins squeezed by greater competition and they are also forced to raise more capital to comply with stiffer regulatory requirements.

Maintaining return on equity on the higher capital base becomes difficult, so banks resort to risky lending. This creates conditions for a crisis. This has not happened in India for a number of reasons which include prudent economic management, the steady improvement in growth in the Indian economy and sound regulation.

An important contributory factor, in our view, is public ownership of banks. In what ways can public ownership contribute to stability in banking? We would put forward a few tentative reasons:

- Government ownership makes for public confidence in the safety of deposits and this is a stabilizing factor in times of broader economic distress or when a PSB is in a stressed situation.
- PSBs tend to be risk-averse compared to private banks or foreign banks; this could be because incentives for taking higher risk are absent. Risk-aversion limits the upside potential in terms of performance and results in relative underperformance. However, it also limits the downside, the probability of failure. Heterogeneity in risk management models used in a financial system is said to contribute to stability of the system. Likewise, diversity in ownership and hence in risk appetites appears to make for stability.
- The relative underperformance of PSBs would itself be a source of instability if the gap with respect to private banks was too large and persistent. This has not been the case in Indian banking. For most of the postreform period, PSBs have shown a trend toward improvement in performance. Thus,

stability in banking has been accompanied by a trend toward improvement in efficiency. Overall, the system appears to have achieved the right trade-off between efficiency and stability.

- There are statutory checks on executive malfeasance through institutions such as the Central Vigilance Commission and the Comptroller and Auditor General.
- When an economy is passing through difficult times, banks suffer an erosion in capital. It is difficult for a private bank to top up its capital in such times by accessing funds from the market. The bank may have to reduce its balance sheet ("de-leveraging"). Or the bank may have to take risky bets in order to boost performance and capital. Either course jeopardizes systemic stability. The government can, however, infuse capital into PSBs from its budget in the confidence that better times will return. Thus, government ownership of banks can be a source of stability in lean times.

In Chapter 1, we quoted the Vickers Commission in the United Kingdom as saying that it was worth incurring a cost of up to 3 percent of GDP every year in order to prevent a 5-percent chance of a financial crisis—the cost imposed by a financial crisis, when it happens, is greater than that.

In India, the cumulative cost of recapitalization of PSBs amounts to less than 0.5 percent of the average GDP over 1994 to 2015, a period of over two decades. The cost of recapitalization, it would seem, has been miniscule going by the Vickers Commission norm. It was a cost eminently worth paying, given that the Indian banking system has not faced a crisis in the period.

Government ownership of banks, like government ownership of any business, is seen as hugely negative. Ownership by government is perceived as coming in the way of long-term financial performance because governments have objectives other than profit and politicians and bureaucrats cannot resist the temptation to meddle in government-owned companies at the cost of financial performance.

The Indian experience with PSBs belies this view. When government-owned banks are subject to market discipline—by being exposed to competition and listed on the stock exchanges—it appears to limit the scope for political or bureaucratic interference. There are institutional and retail investors to whom PSBs and the government are accountable. We have seen what the long-term outcomes are. Efficiency has improved over a long period and the system has been stable. Government ownership, it would seem, is compatible with efficiency and stability in banking.

Banking everywhere has a quasi-government element to it. Banking systems go through periodic crises during which governments acquire ownership in varying degrees in banks. When the economies and banks recover, governments divest their holdings in banks and the banks again become wholly private-owned—until the next crisis starts.

The Indian experience suggests that there may be a case for having some component of government ownership permanently in banking. Such ownership could be a source of stability.

Summary

By some indicators, banks in the advanced economies have become stronger than during the financial crisis of 2007. However, concentration in banking has increased and the TBTF problem remains unresolved. We are not sure, therefore, that another financial crisis is unlikely.

Many economists and policy-makers are of the view that tinkering at the margins will not help produce a safer world of banking. We need radical, out-of-the-box solutions. Economists Mian and Sufi think the key is to keep household debt within limits and to move toward SRMs where borrowers share the downside as well as the upside to housing prices with lenders.

Adrian Turner, former head of the FSA, thinks that we must control the quantity as well as mix of credit. Doing so would require us to control the drivers of credit, such as real estate, inequality and global imbalances, and setting risk weights for various sectors that reflect the social cost of lending to these sectors, not merely the private costs.

Mervyn King, former Governor of the Bank of England, favors the central bank acting as a PFAS. Banks would know in advance how much funds against the assets they hold—this is a measure of their liquid assets. The liquid assets must always exceed their liquid liabilities. In other words, banks can raise deposits only to an extent where they have enough liquid assets to cover the deposits.

The Indian experience with banking shows that it is possible to have the right trade-off between efficiency and stability in banking by having government-owned banks in the system alongside private banks. Given that incentives in risk-taking in PSBs are somewhat muted, having a mix of government and private ownership might well conduce to stability in the system.

Notes

Chapter 1

1. Caprio and Klingebiel (1996).
2. Boyd et al. (2000).
3. Calomiris and Haber (2014, pp. 10–12).
4. Dell' Ariccia, Detragiache, and Rajan (2008, pp. 89–112).
5. Mian and Sufi (2015).
6. Laeven and Valencia (2012).
7. Reinhart and Rogoff (2011).
8. Reinhart and Rogoff (2011, p. 164).
9. Reinhart and Rogoff (2011, p. 147).
10. Reinhart and Rogoff (2011, p. 154).
11. Reinhart and Rogoff (2011, p. 225).
12. Honovan and Klingebiel (2000).
13. Boyd, Kwak, and Smith (2005, pp. 977–99).
14. Vickers (2011).
15. The Financial Crisis Inquiry Report (2011, p. 215).
16. The Financial Crisis Inquiry Report (2011, p. 215).
17. The Financial Crisis Inquiry Report (2011, p. 222).
18. Congressional Budget Office (2013).
19. Laeven and Valencia (2012).
20. Congressional Budget Office (2013, p. 18).
21. Reinhart and Rogoff (2011, p. 26).
22. Ball (2014).

Chapter 2

1. Shiller (2008, p. 32).
2. Shiller (2008, p. 41).
3. Rajan (2010, p. 24).
4. Kiviat (2010).
5. Rajan (2010, pp. 32–41).
6. The Financial Crisis Inquiry Commission Report (2011).
7. The Financial Crisis Inquiry Commission Report (2011, p. 41).
8. Rajan (2010, p. 36).

9. The Financial Crisis Inquiry Commission Report (2011, p. 454).

10. The Financial Crisis Inquiry Commission Report (2011, p. xxvii).

11. The Financial Crisis Inquiry Commission Report (2011, p. 454).

12. Mae and Mac (2014).

13. The Financial Crisis Inquiry Commission Report (2011, p. 460).

14. The Financial Crisis Inquiry Commission Report (2011, p. 70).

15. The Financial Crisis Inquiry Commission Report (2011, p. 449).

16. The Financial Crisis Inquiry Commission Report (2011, p. 521).

17. UNCTAD (2009, p. 7).

18. Eichengreen (2010, p. 4).

19. Shiller (2008, p. 48).

20. Shiller (2008, p. 49).

21. Eichengreen (2010, p. 5).

22. Turner (2016, p. 20).

23. Turner (2016, p. 25).

24. Sahay et al. (2015).

25. Financial Services Authority (2009, pp. 39–49).

26. The Financial Crisis Inquiry Commission Report (2011, p. xx).

27. Calomiris and Haber (2014, pp. 260–61).

28. The Financial Crisis Inquiry Commission Report (2011, p. xxvi).

29. The Financial Crisis Inquiry Commission Report (2011, p. xxvi).

30. Haldane (2009).

31. The Financial Crisis Inquiry Commission Report (2011, p. 11).

32. The Financial Crisis Inquiry Commission Report (2011, p. 88).

33. The Financial Crisis Inquiry Commission Report (2011, p. xii).

34. The Financial Crisis Inquiry Commission Report (2011, p. 428).

35. IMF (2008, p. 31).

36. The Financial Crisis Inquiry Commission Report (2011, p. 19).

37. The Financial Crisis Inquiry Commission Report (2011, p. 71).

38. The Financial Crisis Inquiry Commission Report (2011, pp. 127–29).

39. The Financial Crisis Inquiry Commission Report (2011, pp. xxv).

40. White (2010, pp. 211–26).

41. The Financial Crisis Inquiry Commission Report (2011, p. xxv).

42. "A Fine Too Far, The Economist" (2015).

43. The Financial Crisis Inquiry Commission Report (2011, p. 67).

44. The Financial Crisis Inquiry Commission Report (2011, p. 70).

45. The Financial Crisis Inquiry Commission Report (2011, p. 70).

46. The Financial Crisis Inquiry Commission Report (2011, p. 85).

47. The Financial Crisis Inquiry Commission Report (2011, pp. 86–87).

48. The Financial Crisis Inquiry Commission Report (2011, p. 110).

49. The Financial Crisis Inquiry Commission Report (2011, p. 110).

50. The Financial Crisis Inquiry Commission Report (2011, p. xx).

51. The Financial Crisis Inquiry Commission Report (2011, pp. 91–92).
52. The Financial Crisis Inquiry Commission Report (2011, p. 34).
53. The Financial Crisis Inquiry Commission Report (2011, p. 35).
54. The Financial Crisis Inquiry Commission Report (2011, p. 55).
55. The Financial Crisis Inquiry Commission Report (2011, p. 11).
56. The Financial Crisis Inquiry Commission Report (2011, p. 92).
57. The Financial Crisis Inquiry Commission Report (2011, pp. 113–44).
58. The Financial Crisis Inquiry Commission Report (2011, p. 101).
59. The Financial Crisis Inquiry Commission Report (2011, p. 48).
60. The Financial Crisis Inquiry Commission Report (2011, p. 227).
61. Mian and Sufi (2014).
62. Mian and Sufi (2014, pp. 4–8).
63. Mian and Sufi (2014, pp. 20–24).
64. Mian and Sufi (2014, pp. 33–34).
65. Mian and Sufi (2014, p. 77).
66. Mian and Sufi (2014, p. 79).
67. Mian and Sufi (2014, p. 83).
68. Mian and Sufi (2014, pp. 87–88).

Chapter 3

1. Basel Committee on Banking Supervision (2010a).
2. Target practice (2009).
3. Admati and Hellwig (2013).
4. Basel Committee on Banking Supervision (2010b).
5. Basel Committee on Banking Supervision (2013).
6. Gomes and Khan (2011).
7. A Review of Corporate Governance in UK banks and Other Financial Industry Entities (2009, p. 13).
8. Report of the Parliamentary Commission on Banking Standards (2013, p. 327).
9. Report of the Parliamentary Commission on Banking Standards (2013, p. 329).
10. Report of the Parliamentary Commission on Banking Standards (2013, pp. 330–43).
11. Report of the Parliamentary Commission on Banking Standards (2013, p. 341).
12. The Independent (2016).
13. Report of the Parliamentary Commission on Banking Standards (2013, p. 312).
14. Report of the Parliamentary Commission on Banking Standards (2013, p. 365).

15. Report of the Parliamentary Commission on Banking Standards (2013, pp. 127–28).
16. Angeli and Gitay (2015).
17. "Tilting the Level Playing Field" (2013).
18. Binham Caroline, Regulators plan to extend bank bonus clawback to 10 years, www.ft.com/cms/s/0/3e65d76c-198b-11e5-a130-2e7db721f996.html
19. Jacome and Nier (2012).
20. The Economist, "Credit and Blame" (2007).
21. Daniel I (2009).
22. Schwarcz (2016).
23. Priewe (2010, pp. 37–39).
24. Priewe (2010, p. 41).
25. "Report of the Commission of Experts of the President of the United Nations General Assembly on Reforms of the International Monetary and Financial System" (2009, p. 90).
26. "Report of the Commission of Experts of the President of the United Nations General Assembly on Reforms of the International Monetary and Financial System" (2009, p. 92).
27. Financial Services Authority (2009, p. 97).

Chapter 4

1. Laeven, Ratnovski, and Tong (2014).
2. Barth and Sau (2014).
3. King (2016, location: 543).
4. King (2016, location: 1398).
5. King (2016, location: 1439).
6. Report of the Parliamentary Commission on Banking Standards (2013, p. 112).
7. Saunders and Cornett (2013, p. 495).
8. Haldane (2012, p. 9).
9. Hughes and Mester (2013).
10. Report of the Parliamentary Commission on Banking Standards (2013, p. 114).
11. Report of the Parliamentary Commission on Banking Standards (2013, p. 115).
12. Haldane (2012, pp. 2–3).
13. Haldane (2012, p. 3).
14. Report of the Parliamentary Commission on Banking Standards (2013, p. 114).
15. King (2016, location: 1467).

16. Haldane (2012, p. 4).
17. Rajan (2010, p. 195).
18. Johnson (2013).
19. Kashkari (2016).
20. Chow and Surti (2011).
21. Chow and Surti (2011).
22. The Independent Commission on Banking (2011).
23. The Independent Commission on Banking (2011, p. 112).
24. Noam Noked, Does Volcker+ Vickers- Liikanen, March 8, 2014 https://corpgov.law.harvard.edu/2014/03/08/does-volcker-vickers-liikanen
25. Haldane (2012, p. 6).
26. Haldane (2012, p. 7).
27. Johnson (2016).
28. King (2016, location: 1770).
29. Levine (2016).

Chapter 5

1. Forbes (2015), "A Look at Common Equity Tier 1 Capital Ratios for the Largest U.S. Banks."
2. Nouy Daniele (2016), www.bankingsupervision.europa.eu/press/speeches/date/2016/html/se160406.en.html
3. Ryan and Borak (2016).
4. Wall Street Journal (2016), "Most European Banks Survive Stress Test," www.wsj.com/articles/most-european-banks-pass-stress-test-1469824257
5. Mian and Sufi (2015).
6. Mian and Sufi (2015, p. 150).
7. Mian and Sufi (2015, p. 141).
8. Mian and Sufi (2015, pp. 137–38).
9. Mian and Sufi (2015, pp. 170–174).
10. Mian and Sufi (2015, pp. 174–178, 180–184).
11. Turner (2016).
12. Turner (2016, pp. 186–94).
13. Turner (2016, pp. 175–84).
14. Turner (2016, pp. 195–209).
15. King (2016, location: 3842).
16. King (2016, location: 3855–3865).
17. King (2016, location: 3965).
18. King (2016, location: 3982).
19. Jonathan McMillan, www.endofbanking.org/the-end-of-alchemy-by-mervyn-king-a-critical-book-review-1-18117154/.

20. "Germany: Technical Note on Banking Structure" (2011).
21. The Economist, "Special Report on International Banking" (2010).
22. Report on Trend and Progress in Banking and RBI (2014–15).
23. "Financial Stability Report" (2014).
24. Demirgüç-Kunt and Detragiache (1998).

References

Admati, A., and M. Hellwig. 2013. *The Bankers' New Clothes: What's Wrong with Banking and What To Do About It*. Princeton: Princeton University.

"A Fine Too Far." 2015. *The Economist*, February 4, Retrieved from www.economist.com/news/business-and-finance/21642130-justice-departments-treatment-sp-raises-some-serious-questions-fine-too-far

"A Look at Common Equity Tier 1 Capital Ratios for the Largest U.S. Banks." 2015. *Forbes*, March 6. www.forbes.com/sites/greatspeculations/2015/03/06/a-look-at-common-equity-tier-1-capital-ratios-for-the-largest-u-s-banks/#b46e3836945f

Angeli, M., and S. Gitay. 2015. "Bonus Regulation: Aligning Reward with Risk in the Banking Sector." *Bank of England Quarterly Bulletin*, p. Q4.

A Review of Corporate Governance in UK Banks and Other Financial Industry Entities. June 2009. p. 13. http://webarchive.nationalarchives.gov.uk/+/http:/www.hm-treasury.gov.uk/d/walker_review_261109.pdf

Assembly on Reforms of the International Monetary and Financial System." 2009. United Nations, New York.

Ball, L.M. 2014. "Long-Term Damage from the Great Recession in the OECD Countries." NBER Working Paper 20185.

Barbara, K. 2010. "Economic Seer Says U.S. Not Addressing Cause of Crisis." *Time*, May 21. Retrieved from http://content.time.com/time/business/article/0,8599,1989916,00.html

Barth, J.R., and M. Sau. 2014. "The Big Keep Getting Bigger: Too-Big-to-Fail Banks 30 Years Later." *Center for Financial Markets*. US: Milken Institute.

"Basel Committee on Banking Supervision." 2010a. *Basel* III: *A Global Regulatory Framework for More Resilient Banks and Banking Systems*, Retrieved from www.bis.org/publ/bcbs189.pdf

"Basel Committee on Banking Supervision." 2010b. *An Assessment of the Long-Term Economic Impact of Stronger Capital and Liquidity Requirements*. Retrieved from www.bis.org/publ/bcbs173.pdf

"Basel Committee on Banking Supervision." 2013. *Basel* III: *The Liquidity Coverage Ratio and Liquidity Risk Monitoring Tools*. Retrieved from www.bis.org/publ/bcbs238.pdf

Binham Caroline, Regulators plan to extend bank bonus clawback to 10 years, www.ft.com/cms/s/0/3e65d76c-198b-11e5-a130-2e7db721f996.html

Boyd, J.H., S. Kwak, and B. Smith. 2005. "The Real Output Losses Associated with Modern Banking Crises." *Journal of Money, Credit and Banking* 37, no. 6, pp. 977–99.

Boyd, J.H., P. Gumis, S. Kawak, and B.D. Smith. 2000. "A User's Guide to Banking Crises." Retrieved from www.worldbank.org/finance/assets/images/depins05.pdf

Calomiris, C.W., and S.H. Haber. 2014. *Fragile by Design: The Political Origins of Banking Crises and Scarce Credit*, 10–12. 6 Vols. Princeton: Princeton University Press.

Caprio, G., and D. Klingebiel. 1996. "Bad Insolvency: Bad Luck, Bad Policy or Bad Banking?" In *Proceedings of the Annual World Bank Conference on Development Economics*, eds., M. Bruno and B. Plekovic, 79–104. Washington, DC: World Bank.

Changing Banking for Good, Report of the Parliamentary Commission on Banking Standards. UK. p. 327. http://www.parliament.uk/documents/banking-commission/Banking-final-report-volume-i.pdf and http://www.parliament.uk/documents/banking-commission/Banking-final-report-vol-ii.pdf

Chow, J.T., and J. Surti. 2011. "Making Banks Safer: Can Volcker and Vickers Do It?" IMF Working Paper, pp. 1–34.

Congressional Budget Office, Financial Regulatory Reform: Financial Crisis Losses and Potential Impacts of the Dodd-Frank Act, January 2013.

"Credit and Blame." 2007. *The Economist*, September 6. Retrieved from www.economist.com/node/9769471

Daniel, I. 2009. "Three Suggestions for Reforming Rating Agencies." *The Atlantic*, Retrieved from www.theatlantic.com/business/archive/2009/06/three-suggestions-for-reforming-rating-agencies/19784/

Dell' Ariccia, G., E. Detragiache, and R. Rajan. 2008. "The Real Effect of Banking Crises." *Journal of Financial Intermediation* 17, no. 1, pp. 89–112.

Demirgüç-Kunt, A., and E. Detragiache. 1998. "Financial Liberalisation and Financial Fragility." *Annual World Bank Conference on Development Economics*, Fostering Growth While Containing Risk, Yale University.

Eichengreen, B. 2010. "Macroeconomic and Financial Policies Before and After the Crisis." In *East-West Center/KDI Conference on the Global Economic Crisis*, Honolulu, 19–20 August, p. 4. Berkeley: University of California.

Financial Services Authority. 2009. "A Regulatory Response to the Global Banking Crisis." pp. 39–49.

"Financial Stability Report." December 2014. RBI.

"Germany: Technical Note on Banking Structure." December 2011. IMF Country Report No 11/370. www.imf.org/external/pubs/ft/scr/2011/cr11370.pdf

Gomes, T., and N. Khan. 2011. "Strengthening Bank Management of Liquidity Risk." *Bank of Canada, Financial System Review* 5, pp. 35–42.

Haldane, A.G. 2009. *Banking on the State*. Paper Delivered at the Federal Reserve Bank of Chicago Twelfth Annual International Banking Conference on "The International Financial Crisis: Have the Rules Changed?," September 25.

Haldane, A.G. 2012. "On Being the Right Size." The 2012 Beesley Lectures, at the Honovan, P., and D. Klingebiel. 2000. "Controlling Fiscal Costs of Banking Crises." www.worldbank.org/finance/assets/images/depins02.pdf

Hughes, J.P., and L.J. Mester. 2013. "Who Said Large Banks Don't Experience Scale Economies? Evidence from a Risk-Return-Driven Cost Function." Working Paper No. 13–13, Research Department, Federal Reserve Bank of Philadelphia.

https://corpgov.law.harvard.edu/2014/03/08/does-volcker-vickers-liikanen

IMF 2008. *Global Financial Stability Report*, p. 31.

Institute of Directors, London. (This article surveys some of the evidence on this topic).

Jacome, L., and E.W. Nier. 2012. "Macroprudential Policy: Protecting the Whole." IMF Finance and Development.

Johnson, S. 2013. "The Myth of a Perfect Orderly Liquidation Authority for Big Banks." *New York Times*, Retrieved from http://economix.blogs.nytimes.com/2013/05/16/the-myth-of-a-perfect-orderly-liquidation-authority-for-big-banks/?_r=0

Johnson, S. 2016. "A Size Cap for the Largest U.S. Banks." *Federal Reserve Bank of Minneapolis Symposium on Ending Too Big To Fail*, April 18.

Jonathan McMillan, www.endofbanking.org/the-end-of-alchemy-by-mervyn-king-a-critical-book-review-1-18117154/

Kashkari, N. 2016. "An Update on Ending Too Big to Fail." The *Third Symposium on Ending Too Big to Fail*, Peterson Institute, Washington, D.C. Federal Reserve Bank of Minneapolis. www.minneapolisfed.org/news-and-events/presidents-speeches/an-update-on-ending-too-big-to-fail

King, M. 2016. *The End of Alchemy: Money, Banking and the Future of the Global Economy*. Kindle Edition. NewYork: WW Norton & Company.

Laeven, L., and F. Valencia. 2012. "Systemic Banking Crises Database: An Update." IMF Working Paper.

Laeven, L., L. Ratnovski, and H. Tong. 2014. "Bank Size and Systemic Risk." *IMF Staff Discussion Note*.

Levine, R. 2016. "Perspectives on Breaking Up the Big Banks." *Federal Reserve Bank of Minneapolis Symposium on Ending Too Big To Fail*.

Mae, F., and F. Mac. 2014. "Structurally Unsound." *The Economist*, October 25. Retrieved from www.economist.com/news/finance-and-economics/21627699-america-restores-weak-lending-standards-led-housing

Mian, A., and A. Sufi. 2014. *The House of Debt*. Chicago and London: The University of Chicago Press.

Mian, A., and A. Sufi. 2015. *The House of Debt*. Princeton: Princeton University Press.

Nouy, D. 2016. www.bankingsupervision.europa.eu/press/speeches/date/2016/html/se160406.en.html

Priewe, J. December 2010. "What Went Wrong? Alternative Explanations of the Global Crisis." In UNCTAD, *The Financial and Economic Crisis of 2008–09 and Developing Countries*, eds. S. Dullien, D.J. Kotte, and A. Márquez, 37–39. New York and Geneva: United Nations, December 2010.

Rajan, R. 2010. *Fault Lines: How Hidden Fractures Still Threaten the World Economy*, 24. Princeton: Princeton University Press.

Reinhart, C., and K. Rogoff. 2011. *This Time Is Different: Eight Centuries of Financial Folly*. Princeton: Princeton University Press.

"Report of the Commission of Experts of the President of the United Nations General "Special Report on International Banking." 2010. *The Economist*, May 13.

Report on Trend and Progress in Banking and RBI. 2014–2015. website, Reserve Bank of India.

Ryan, T., and D. Borak. 2016. "Fed Stress Tests Clear 31 of 33 Big U.S. Banks to Boost Returns to Investors." *The Wall Street Journal*, June 29. www.wsj.com/articles/fed-stress-tests-clear-31-of-33-big-u-s-banks-for-capital-returns-1467232237

Sahay, R., M. Čihák, P. N'Diaye, A. Barajas. 2015. "Rethinking Financial Deepening: Stability and Growth in Emerging Markets." *Revista de Economía Institucional* 17, no. 33, pp. 73–107.

Saunders, A., and M.M. Cornett. 2013. *Financial Institutions Management: A Risk Management Approach*, 495. New Delhi: McGraw Hill. (The authors survey several papers on this topic).

Schwarcz, S.L. 2016. "Securitization and Post-Crisis Financial Regulation." *Cornell Law Review Online* 101, p. 115.

Shiller, R. 2008. *The Sub-Prime Solution: How Today's Global Financial Crisis Happened and What to Do About It*, 32. Princeton: Princeton University Press.

Stephanie, B. 2016. "The Financial Crisis Inquiry Commission Report, Financial Report of the National Commission on the Causes of the Financial and Economic Crisis in the United States. Retrieved from http://cybercemetery.unt.edu/archive/fcic/20110310172443/http://fcic.gov/

"Target Practice." 2009. *The Economist*, July 9. Retrieved from www.economist.com/node/13998740

The Financial Crisis Inquiry Report 2011: Final Report of the National Commission on the Causes of the Financial and Economic Crisis in the United States. www.gpo.gov/fdsys/pkg/GPO-FCIC/pdf/GPO-FCIC.pdf

"The Independent Commission on Banking. 2011." *Final Report*, September. Retrieved from www.ecgi.org/documents/icb_final_report_12sep2011.pdf

"Theresa May's Plan to Put Workers on Boards Is Borrowed from Germany and France." *The Independent*, July 12, 2016. Retrieved from www.independent. co.uk/news/business/news/theresa-may-board-corporate-plan-germany-france-productivity-economics-a7132221.html

"Tilting the Level Playing Field." 2013. *The Economist*, March 7. Retrieved from www.economist.com/news/finance-and-economics/21573122-regime-change-europe-tilting-playing-field

Turner, A. 2016. *Between Debt and the Devil: Money, Credit and Fixing Global Finance*. Princeton: Princeton University Press.

UNCTAD. 2009. p. 7.

Vickers, J. 2011. *Independent Commission on Banking*. UK: The Stationery Office. http://webarchive.nationalarchives.gov.uk/20131003105424/https:/hmt-sanctions.s3.amazonaws.com/ICB%20final%20report/ICB%2520Final%2520Report[1].pdf

Wall Street Journal. 2016. "Most European Banks Survive Stress Test." www.wsj. com/articles/most-european-banks-pass-stress-test-1469824257

White, L.J. 2010. The Credit Rating Agencies." *Journal of Economic Perspectives* 24, no. 2, pp. 211–226.

Index

OTHER TITLES IN OUR FINANCE AND FINANCIAL MANAGEMENT COLLECTION

John A. Doukas, Old Dominion University, Editor

- *Essentials of Retirement Planning: A Holistic Review of Personal Retirement Planning Issues and Employer-Sponsored Plans, Third Edition* by Eric J. Robbins
- *Financial Services Sales Handbook: A Professionals Guide to Becoming a Top Producer* by Clifton T. Warren
- *Money Laundering and Terrorist Financing Activities: A Primer on Avoidance Management for Money Managers* by Milan Frankl and Ayse Ebru Kurcer
- *Introduction to Foreign Exchange Rates, Second Edition* by Thomas J. O'Brien
- *Rays of Research on Real Estate Development* by Jaime Luque
- *Weathering the Storm: The Financial Crisis and the EU Response, Volume I: Background and Origins of the Crisis* by Javier Villar Burke
- *Weathering the Storm: The Financial Crisis and the EU Response, Volume II: The Response to the Crisis* by Javier Villar Burke
- *Rethinking Risk Management: Critically Examining Old Ideas and New Concepts* by Rick Nason

Announcing the Business Expert Press Digital Library

Concise e-books business students need for classroom and research

This book can also be purchased in an e-book collection by your library as

- a one-time purchase,
- that is owned forever,
- allows for simultaneous readers,
- has no restrictions on printing, and
- can be downloaded as PDFs from within the library community.

Our digital library collections are a great solution to beat the rising cost of textbooks. E-books can be loaded into their course management systems or onto students' e-book readers. The **Business Expert Press** digital libraries are very affordable, with no obligation to buy in future years. For more information, please visit **www.businessexpertpress.com/librarians**. To set up a trial in the United States, please email **sales@businessexpertpress.com**.

www.ingramcontent.com/pod-product-compliance
Lightning Source LLC
Chambersburg PA
CBHW072342200326
41519CB00015B/3634